FEARFULLY FEMALE

AND

WONDERFULLY WOMAN

BECOMING ALL THAT GOD CREATED

Cinthia W. Pratt, MA

WESTBOW
PRESS
A DIVISION OF THOMAS NELSON

WestBow Press books may be ordered through booksellers or by contacting:

WestBow Press
A Division of Thomas Nelson
1663 Liberty Drive
Bloomington, IN 47403
www.westbowpress.com
1-(866) 928-1240

ISBN: 978-1-4497-1675-2 (sc)
ISBN: 978-1-4497-1677-6 (hc)
ISBN: 978-1-4497-1676-9 (e)

Library of Congress Control Number: 2011928730

Printed in the United States of America

WestBow Press rev. date: 05/05/2011

To Doug, the absolute love of my life and to all the members of my Encouragement Entourage... Fearfully Wonderful women every one.

ACKNOWLEDGEMENTS

This book could not have been written without the abundant grace of God and the constant inspiration and guidance of the Holy Spirit. I praise my Savior for leading me gently through each twist and turn and for patiently guiding my steps along this solitary path of attempting to put on page what he has placed within my heart.

I also thank my loving husband and friend, Doug, for his courage to believe in my purpose, for his patience with my doubt and insecurity, and for his never- waning encouragement and support. He is sincerely the love of my life.

And finally, to **all** the fearfully wonderful women in my life who would not allow me to become weary in well doing. You provided clarity to my thinking, encouragement for my steps and laughter throughout the journey. At the end of this project, I find that I did not come alone. The members of my encouragement entourage have been with me every step of the way.

CONTENTS

CHAPTER 1

A few Traveling Tips Before we start

Psalm 139:14 reads: *"I will praise you, for I am fearfully and wonderfully made; marvelous are your works, and my soul knows very well."* The original Hebrew translation for the word "fearfully" as used in this verse is: *with great reverence and heart-felt interest and respect*; while the Hebrew word translated 'wonderfully' in this Biblical text literally means: *unique, set apart or uniquely marvelous* (Zodhiates, 1992).

Sadly most women today cannot honestly declare along with the psalmist that they praise their God because He made them in great reverence with a heart- felt interest and respect for his creation and then set them apart as being uniquely marvelous. Many have not yet realized that they are *fearfully* female and *wonderfully* woman .They cannot in complete honesty state that their soul **knows** the fact of their *marvelous ness* very well. Why do you suppose this is?

I believe that the answer to that question lies at least in part in the fact that for the Christian female, the journey into womanhood and that of moving from little girl to fully woman occurs while living in a world that is not our home and within a culture that does not reflect the norms and values of Christian teaching. We are ambassadors, strangers and aliens on a journey with a final destination and all these many stations and rest stops that we encounter along the way are not our journey's end. Each of us must carefully balance living here in this present culture while seeking to reflect the norms and values of our permanent home: God's heavenly kingdom. We should not be surprised then to find ourselves confused or in culture shock as we navigate our way through the myriad messages being sent through media, peer groups, social institutions and religious systems regarding what it means to be "woman". Whether we are moving from false eyelashes to hot flashes, from flats to first stilettos, from thongs to granny panties, or even from lipstick and mascara to a precision set of tweezers and a good magnifying mirror; we can choose to either eliminate the baggage that we may have acquired along the way or continue to be weighed down by the excess load.

If we believe and desire to follow the teachings of Christ then we must recognize that we are called to be *in the world* and yet not *of the world*. John 15:18-19 reminds us that Christ chose us out of the world and just as the world hated him , when we decide to follow him, it will hate us as well.

> *"If the world hates you, keep in mind that it hated me first. If you belonged to the world, it would love you as its own. As it is, you do not belong to the world, but I have chosen you out of the world. That is why the world hates you."- John 15:18-19*

So, what's a girl to do? How do we reflect the values and principles of our heavenly home while living, growing and interacting in this present culture? How do we choose which messages we will accept and carry with us and which we will leave behind? How do we turn down the many clamoring voices of this present world to hear the often stifled and quiet voice of our Lord? Wouldn't it be great if together as women we could eliminate all the excess baggage that weighs us down and be forewarned of the twists and turns that lie in the road up ahead? That was the goal in writing this book. The author is inviting all women regardless of their status, age or phase of life to determine to be all that God created them to be, and to dare to be fearfully female and wonderfully woman.

Taking this challenge to join one another in the journey of a life time will require being willing to turn down the voices shouting lies and half-truths aimed at distorting God's perfect plan so that we might hear the wonderful truth that our creator has to say. It may also require some of us to take a second look at once widely accepted and unquestioned positions in order to gain a fresh perspective or new insight.

As we journey through the pages of this book, we will examine the messages and lies being hurled at us from the various cultural outlets against the truths that are contained within the scripture and in the kingdom principles established by our creator; then, perhaps as fellow sojourners we can help each other unpack those heavy and entirely unnecessary burdens that have been placed on us by the world systems of media, politics, religion, and gender stereotypes. Hopefully we will have a good time taking an honest look at ourselves, laughing in the full length mirror and learning to accept our flaws while embracing the truth that the female being was created with intent by God and perfectly equipped to perform His divine will. Along the way we will learn the source of our greatest value and deepest pleasure comes from being uniquely His and His uniquely.

Mapping our course and plotting our route

While it is true that many of us enjoy getting in the car on a Sunday afternoon for a leisurely drive with no intended destination; it is also true that coming back home at the end of that leisure is a destination in and of itself. Even impromptu Sunday drives must begin somewhere and take at least a little bit of planning and preparation. At a minimum, our car will need gas or our bicycle tires need to be inflated properly. Even if we are simply out for a stroll, we will need a good pair of walking shoes to go any distance and we will need to agree upon which way to turn as we head out of the driveway. Traveling partners and walking buddies desiring to travel together will be unable to do so without at least deciding upon a shared direction and a final destination. They cannot share their journey if each walks out the door and heads off in an opposite direction nor can they know when their journey is complete if they haven't established a stopping point. If we are going to travel together in this trip of a lifetime , then it seems that the most logical place to begin our planning is in determining where it is we would like to go and then mapping out our shared route and plotting the best course.

Our Starting Point

This book will draw its definitions and images of 'female' from the written and inspired word of the One who created us. Travelers will gather life instructions for the journey ahead from the One who prepared us in advance to complete this journey in a manner that pleases Him. Logically, if a woman does not acknowledge the existence of God then she has no interest in what God has to say about her or about the purpose of her life.

Likewise, it is the perspective of this book that true freedom is found in relationship not in religiosity and that a woman's life purpose cannot be found in marking check lists, jumping through hoops or through any other performance orientation. Sadly, religious dogma, rituals and rules have done much to contribute to the oppression and subjugation of women and some of the strongest lies related to the status and importance of women have come to her under the guise of religious instruction. Therefore, this book is not intended to be a rule book, an agenda, a self-help guide, or as a set of standards for others to duplicate. It does not offer a twelve step plan nor does it suggest a legalistic one size fits all approach to defining what it is to be female.

Alternately, the information contained in this book is shared to encourage every woman to hear the voice of the Lord for herself, to search out scripture for herself, and to decide for herself when the Holy Spirit is speaking directly to her. Ephesians 2:10 tells us that: *"we are God's workmanship, created in Christ Jesus to do good works, which God prepared in advance for us to do"*. This affirmation comes to us right after Paul declared in Ephesians 2:8-9 that: *"it is by grace that you have been saved, through faith—and this not from yourselves, it is the gift of God—not by works, so that no one can boast"*. We may conclude from Paul's words that legalism and strict adherence to laws and regulations does not bring salvation or offer God's grace.

While the truths contained within this book regarding the cultural lies, myths and half-truths being circulated about females could probably be agreed upon by many different perspectives and embraced by varied social and political agendas; the offered solutions contained within these pages for freeing oneself from the bondage of those lies can only be followed by women desiring to be true Disciples of Christ. This book is written from the position that freedom from these long established lies and from the bondage and oppression of women that these lies propagate can only be found by replacing them with total truth. After all, isn't a half -truth nothing but yet another lie? Jesus Christ proclaimed that He is **the** truth in John 14:6:

> *Jesus answered, "I am the way and the truth and the life.*
> *No one comes to the Father except through me".*

He also stated that knowing the truth was the key to our total freedom in John 8:32.

"Then you will know the truth, and the truth will set you free."

It seems obvious then that for any woman to begin the journey toward being a fearful female and a wonderful woman she must start with a personal relationship with Jesus Christ. That relationship is the vital shared starting point for all sojourners wishing to benefit from the perspective followed in this book. The freedom and life being offered within these pages is only obtainable and explainable through the miraculous life giving truth of Jesus Christ. Any woman who cannot agree that truth is only found in Christ will continue exhausting her effort and expiring her energy seeking answers that cannot be found in any other source. Scripture teaches that the battle to be free from bondage cannot be won by any other means.

DETERMINING OUR DESTINATION

Even a leisurely Sunday drive can't last forever and sooner or later every journey ends somewhere. The final stop may not be one that was premeditated or planned but as we all know: "all good things come to an end". According to the Christian faith, the final destination for all Christians is their eternal presence with God in His heavenly Kingdom. Every fearfully wonderful woman of God is on a shared journey toward her heavenly home. If Heaven is the goal, then it is important to establish how someone gets there. Scripture teaches that heaven can only be entered by those who are identified as "Christians". It is important then to know what it means to be a "Christian".

Often times people will declare that they are Christians and seem to know a great deal about the Christian faith without actually being true Christians at all. Their claim to being Christian may be based upon an infant baptism, confirmation, church attendance, having walked down an aisle, having been raised in a religious home, or a host other reasons. They may be able to quote scripture and tell Bible stories quite well. However, having knowledge about a religion or about God and even being able to quote scripture does not establish someone as a Christian. Knowing *about* someone is not the same as personally knowing that person any more than reading a book makes you the friend of the author.

By definition a *Christian* is someone who follows Christ. She would be someone who looks to the teachings of Christ to find meaning and purpose for her life. She is someone who patterns and models her behavior based upon His example and His instructions. She would also be someone who has accepted Christ as her only means of salvation and who has granted Him access to her life as her sovereign Lord (Acts 11:19-26). Her relationship with Christ is a *personal* one rather than one based upon an acquired knowledge set. A personal relationship with someone can only be claimed after the two parties have been acquainted and have established a connection or a bond. A personal relationship also implies doing things together and spending time together. It implies knowing each other and having a report and a sense of sharing or belonging. This is because people who have personal relationships allow each other access into one another's deepest secrets, hopes and desires. They share thoughts, views, dreams and opinions. They also rely upon each other. Church attendance, baptism or involvement in any other religious ritual does not make a person a Christian. Being religious is the not the same as having a personal relationship with God through Christ Jesus. Did you know that God, the creator of the universe, loves you and has a wonderful plan for your life specifically and as an individual? Jeremiah 29:11-13 states:

" For I know the plans I have for you," declares the LORD, "plans to prosper you and not to harm you, plans to give you hope and a future. Then you will call upon me and come and pray to me, and I will listen to you. You will seek me and find me when you seek me with all your heart."

AVOIDING DEAD END ROUTES

One of the greatest differences between Christianity and false religions or false teaching is that Christianity gives sinful humanity hope by offering us the opportunity for a personal relationship with God through His Son Jesus Christ. The God of Christianity loves mankind enough to make a way for an intimate and personal relationship with us. Holy God wants to commune openly with sinful mankind. False religions take away the possibly of a personal, intimate relationship with God by making God impersonal, uninvolved in human affairs and distant or far away. These religions may also make God unapproachable or vengeful and take away the truth of His mercy, compassion and great love.

"But God demonstrates his own love for us, in that while we were still sinners, Christ died for us". Romans 5:8

False religions fall short in helping an individual establish intimate connections with God because having such a relationship cannot about be diminished to simply accepting some new world view or new philosophy of life. Finding God cannot be equated with finding our center or self-actualization. It's actually quite the opposite. Finding God occurs when we come to the end of self and seek something outside ourselves and beyond our control.

Establishing a personal relationship with God isn't about following a set of rules or religious instructions. It's about going in person as an individual to God and talking with Him directly and openly. Because God is total holiness and mankind is sinful He cannot fellowship with us until we admit to our wrong doing and find true forgiveness from Him. We are the ones who committed the wrongful acts and He is the one who has the right to either forgive us or to reject us. A Personal relationship with God begins when we admit that we have sinned against God and that we desire to reestablish a relationship with Him.

"There is no one righteous, not even one" Romans 3:9-10.

"For the wages of sin is death, but the gift of God is eternal life in Christ Jesus our Lord". Romans 6:23

"For all have sinned and fall short of the glory of God," Romans 3:23

The three Scriptures printed above provide a clear picture of the status of mankind in the eyes of Holy God. We are all in this same condition. We have fallen out of relationship with God because we have all broken God's commands. Each of us is a sinner in need of redemption. We all fall short of God's perfect righteousness and none of us can attain the level of holiness that he requires through our own merit. Any religion that offers a works-oriented approach or that suggests a set of rituals and rules that one can follow to achieve relationship with Holy God has no concept of the high debt that is owed Him. No amount of human generosity, good works, virtue or morality, religious activity, charity or civic involvement can gain acceptance with God or buy a person's passage into heaven. We cannot make a bargain with God, offer up an alternative plan or do anything to reconcile ourselves to God and pay the debt owed Him for our sin. It is the lie of a false teaching to suggest that sinful man could ever be good enough or offer up any appeasement to bring about salvation and to reestablish relationship. Isaiah 64:6 makes the short comings of our human attempt at holiness very clear:

*"All of us have become like one who is unclean, and all
our righteous acts are like filthy rags; we all shrivel up like
a leaf, and like the wind our sins sweep us away."*

The works-oriented approach being offered by many false religions would also result in a vicious cycle by demanding that the practitioner keep doing some ritual or moral act to appease God each time they sinned. The presence of sin cancels out holiness. Every time one of God's laws is broken the relationship with God is broken and a new ritual would need to be performed and a new price paid. Most of us find it virtually impossible to go even one day without losing our temper, telling a fib, or thinking an unkind thought. Absolute holiness would not be absolute if it allowed interaction such as this with that which is absolutely holy. Stated another way, any tiny amount of sewage that is released into a glass of crystal clear water contaminates every droplet of liquid that glass contains. All of the water is now impure. Absolute holiness is no longer absolute if there is even a hint of sin present. The endless cycle of breaking laws and then making new atonement for those infractions would never end because our propensity toward sinning would forever continue. Human beings can never be holy without intervention from a being that is already holy.

A truly significant error contained within this works-oriented approach to forgiveness lies in the fact that it is the man-made religious system that is determining the price that God should require for transgressions made against Him. The offended God is not consulted in setting the penalty and cost to appease Him. In essence, the criminal is determining the just penalty for the offense they committed. What type of justice would be delivered by a system that allowed criminals to determine the gravity of their crime and the price they will pay in restitution to society or to the person against whom the crime was committed? How many of us would be willing to allow the person who damaged our property to determine the extent of that damage and what will be paid us in restitution? How many of us would be honest in paying the highest dollar amount possible if we were the party who caused the damage? Is it not human nature to get away with as little effort possible and to barter the lowest price the market will allow?

The desired relationship sinful humanity seeks with Holy God can only be established following His requirements. He is the One who has been offended. It does not matter if someone knows Christ's name and knows everything about The Bible. It doesn't matter if they lead a relatively good life by contributing to charity and supporting social welfare. Following religious rituals and routines better than anyone we know will not gain access for us to God's good graces. Forgiveness and a relationship with God can only happen if we are willing to admit that we are sinners and if we honestly repent from our sinful lifestyle and ask God to forgive us on His terms. The good news is that scripture states that if any of us will admit that we have sinned against God and ask for His forgiveness then He will forgive us.

"If we confess our sins, he is faithful and just and will forgive us our sins and purify us from all unrighteousness". 1 John 1:9

God's terms for relationship are very clearly laid out in His scripture. He requires that each of us as individuals accept the sacrifice of his Son that He made for us.

"For God so loved the world that he gave his one and only Son, that whoever believes in him shall not perish but have eternal life". John 3:16

And this is the testimony: God has given us eternal life, and this life is in his Son. The one who has the Son has this eternal life; the one who does not have the Son of God does not have this eternal life. 1 John 5:11-12

To reject God's sacrifice of His only Son in an attempt to devise our own plan or terms of payment is playing God. Such action suggests we feel that we are in a position to be an equal bargaining partner with God. That is a sin worse that spitting in His face. No created being can be equal to his or her creator. No finite being knows better than an infinite one. God's message is really quite clear cut. He is saying that He will accept any of us as His rightful heir and open up direct access to His throne room if and only if we will recognize Him as sovereign and accept His son Jesus as our Savior. Doing so requires recognizing that you the debt we owe for our transgressions cannot be made right outside of His plan. He is offering to pay that debt which we owe Him for us. His offer is totally free. Holy God loves His creation so much that in an act of absolute undeserved grace and mercy He is extending salvation and redemption through His Son Jesus Christ.

"For it is by grace you have been saved, through faith— and this not from yourselves, it is the gift of God— not by works, so that no one can boast". Ephesians 2:8-9

"How great is the love the Father has lavished on us, that we should be called children of God! And that is what we are! The reason the world does not know us is that it did not know him." 1 John 3:1

"Greater love has no one than this- that he lay down his life for his friends". John 15:13

TAKE CAUTION

Please be warned, the God of the Bible is a righteous and Holy God who demands justice. His judgment will come for all those who reject His mercy and grace. He, Himself, sacrificed Himself for our sins and for the debt that we owe Him so that we might become holy and pure and in turn be able to fellowship with Him eternally. The choice to accept his gift of forgiveness and restoration is ours. God will not force this free gift upon us. We can choose to reject His freely offered plan and face His judgment, or accept His wonderful gift of grace and become His child. Remember, heaven is the home of those who have a personal relationship with Christ Jesus. Access can be gained through no other means. This relationship is freely offered but will never be forced. Each individual woman must decide where she will spend eternity. It all comes down to deciding our life journey's destination for ourselves.

"This day I call heaven and earth as witnesses against you that I have set before you life and death, blessings and curses. Now choose life, so that you and your children may live". Deuteronomy 30:19

COLLECTING TRAVEL DOCUMENTS: COMING TO THE FATHER

There is no special power or magic formula contained in praying the words printed in italics below. Any woman can come to God praying the words of her choosing as long as those words recognize His criteria for salvation and His provision of His son Jesus Christ as the only means to establishing relationship with Him. These words are offered simply to be a guide for anyone who wishes to accept God's gift of grace and who is serious about establishing a relationship with Him but isn't quite sure how to ask. Words similar to the ones contained in the prayer outlined below can be used when a woman has recognized her sin, her need for forgiveness, and her need for a relationship with God through Jesus Christ.

"Father God, I know that I have broken your laws and that I am a sinner. I understand that my sins have separated me from you. I am sincerely repentant for my sin, and now want to turn away from my past sinful life and stubborn disobedience. Please forgive me and give me your free gift of salvation. Restore a right relationship between you and me. I believe and acknowledge that your son, Jesus Christ, lived a sinless life, freely died for my sins, was resurrected from the dead, is alive, and hears this prayer right now. I invite Jesus to be the Lord of my life and to reign in my heart. I ask that as my shepherd He would guide my steps from this day forward. Please send your promised Holy Spirit to teach me your ways and to help me to do your will for the rest of my life. In Jesus' name I pray, Amen."

If you read over the prayer written above and truly believe the words that you read, then you are free to pray that prayer now. You don't need to be at a church or in a meeting. You don't have to wait for a special occasion or even until next Sunday. You don't have to have a preacher or an evangelist present. You don't have to wait until you understand more about the Bible or until you feel better qualified. This is a personal, intimate matter between you and your Creator. Scripture does encourage you, however, to seek out others who are followers of Christ with whom you can share your decision and who can in turn encourage the growth of your faith.

If you did pray that prayer then welcome to the family of God. Praise the Lord as you have been redeemed and the price for your sin has been paid in full. God has accepted you as His child and you now have a personal relationship with Christ. You are at the starting point of the journey to becoming *Fearfully Female and Wonderfully Woman*. Now that we have a shared destination and have established the only route to get there we can continue on our journey together. Welcome traveling companion, now, let's get packing.

✖ ROADSIDE REFLECTIONS:

- Please choose a "stepping our scripture" that you will write as your first claimed promise and record it in your travel journal.

CHAPTER 2

Preparing for the Journey

Preparing for a trip can be a time consuming and arduous task. Considering such things as destination, overall length of the journey, necessary paperwork and shots, travel insurance, security issues, and total costs of the trip can be a serious headache and stressor for even the most seasoned traveler. Experts tell us that the key to traveling well is found in planning, preparing and packing well. In additional to planning primarily for her destination, the skilled traveler will also try to account for every possible detour, diversion, mishap, or lay over along the way. Planning and forethought are vital because while every traveler wants to include all the necessities she may need, she also wants to avoid being unnecessarily delayed, being overburdened or weighed down, and paying additional fees for such things as excess baggage.

Our preparation for the journey through life is much the same as that for any other trip. While, as Christians, we all have a shared final destination for which we long; we also have many stops, unanticipated delays and both enjoyable and less enjoyable detours as we make our way home.

❋ ROADSIDE REFLECTIONS:

- If you were going on a ten day trip that covered various locations with varied climates and activities what would you pack? Remember that baggage costs and that it also weighs you down and slows your pace. What would be the essentials for your journey?

CREATING AN ITINERARY:

In Chapter 1 we already established our shared final destination and determined that there's really only one sure route for arriving there. Though we are all traveling together, we will each need to follow the path that God Himself has prepared for us if we are going to receive the greatest fulfillment and joy. We will have traveling companions who will join us along the way. Some will walk along side us for only one leg of the journey while others will be life companions who will go the distance with us. Some of those who share our journey will be of our choosing while others will not. Some will be enjoyable companions and others will be less encouraging or perhaps downright frustrating for us. God has our perfect path already in mind and has plotted out our itineraries. He has also provided His living word, The Bible, to serve as our guide book. It contains all our necessary travel instructions and other helpful information. Keeping a well read and marked copy of the scripture on hand will help us when we are uncertain or when the path is obscure and twisted. The scripture will serve as a road map to direct our path and will offer insight to shed clear light on the correct direction in which we should go (Psalm 119:105, 2 Timothy 3:16-17).

"You make known to me the path of life;
in your presence there is fullness of joy;
at your right hand are pleasures forevermore."
—*Psalm 16:11*

BOOKING A RESERVATION AND PAYING IN ADVANCE:

Our reservation has been booked and paid in advance through the person of Jesus Christ. Eternal life and a permanent home in heaven were made accessible to us through his shed blood. Any woman who has acknowledged Christ as her savior and has accepted his gift of salvation has a reservation which has been paid in full. Jesus himself is her guarantee of her inheritance and of having a place waiting for her when she arrives in God's Heavenly Kingdom. He is her travel insurance. There is no need to worry any longer about that particular detail of our trip. Our Father has handled it on our behalf.

> *"But our citizenship is in heaven, and from it we await a Savior,*
> *the Lord Jesus Christ, who will transform our lowly body to*
> *be like his glorious body, by the power that enables him even*
> *to subject all things to himself". - Philippians 3:20-21*

TRAVEL SAFETY AND SECURITY:

Those of us who desire to follow Jesus on this remarkable journey need to be certain that we can handle the turbulence, bumpy roads and loss of sleep that might lie ahead. He doesn't want us to agree to travel with him only to change our minds should parts of the journey become less than pleasant. Circumstances of life are going to come our way and being a disciple of Jesus means that we must be willing to follow where he leads regardless of those circumstances or less than pleasant situations that might occur along the way (John 12:25-26). Those who choose to travel with Jesus do have the assurance and security of knowing that in each possible difficulty God has promised not to leave us alone. He promised never to forsake us (Hebrews 13:5). We can trust that God is with us should the storm clouds roll in overhead. He is right beside us when we are frightened or insecure. We can be strong and courageous because the God of the universe is with us (Deuteronomy 31:6). If that one fact is true, then what in this world are the issues and matters over which those who travel with the Lord following his itinerary with him leading the way need to be concerned? After all, Jesus is our G.P.S. (*God Provided Safety, Security, Shelter and Shepherd*). We can trust the Lord in our daily travel whatever it may bring if we can simply remember that He is with us, leading us, instructing us and giving us victory.

> *"For whatsoever is born of God overcometh the world: and this is the*
> *victory that overcometh the world, even our faith."- 1 John 5:4*

> *"The Lord is my light and my salvation; whom shall I fear? The Lord*
> *is the stronghold of my life; of whom shall I be afraid?" -Psalm 27:1*

The traveling companions of Jesus can also be assured that nothing touches our lives that our sovereign God does not know about and has not allowed. Circumstances that are difficult to understand and uncomfortable for us at the moment can be used to achieve His plans and his purposes if we will continue to trust Him (Genesis 50:20). Our Father has already been up the road ahead of us. He knows the path on which we are traveling (Job 23:10, Matthew 6:32). He has clear vision and we can trust Him because He sees and knows so much more than we can possibly see or know (Isaiah 55:8). He is all knowing; God knows what lies ahead and has already made preparation for our successful passage. We may not know where we are going but the one who has called us and is leading us does (Hebrews 11:8). Our God is all sufficient; He is the source of everything that we will need to successfully complete our journey (Philippians 4:19). God is our Abba- daddy; His gentle Father's heart is our comfort for times of uncertainty and question. He is the Author of our faith and is our refuge and strength when we have unbelief or doubt. We can be assured that He will complete what He has started in us (Philippians 1:6). He is our peace when we are in chaos or confusion. He is the source of unconditional and everlasting love to cast out all our fear (1 John 4:18). Our hope is secure because its source is Him. As we move forward in faith He will make the path straight for us and illuminate it with his unfailing presence and unending grace (Job 37:21).

EVALUATING TRAVEL COSTS:

Perhaps the greatest consideration in planning any journey is the cost of the trip. Travel is not an inexpensive venture in this day and age. Many a horror story has been told of an unprepared traveler who gets far from home and in a foreign land only to discover that she does not have the necessary means to cover an emergency or to book a return passage home. The extensive journey upon which we are about to embark is not without great costs and all travelers are advised to carefully consider those costs before committing to this trip.

In Luke 14:28-33 Jesus compares the stories of two men. The first man is building a tower. The second man is a king who is contemplating going to battle. The one thing that both men in this story share in common is the need to carefully consider the costs of their intended engagement.

Jesus ends his parable in verse 33 by reminding his listeners that anyone who desires to be his disciple must likewise count the costs and be willing to give up everything to follow him. Following Christ comes with a high travel fare. It requires the willing surrender of everything to His control and ownership. That is why He tells us to carefully consider the cost of becoming his disciple. Luke 9: 62 reminds us that : "No one who puts his hand to the plow and looks back is fit for service in the kingdom of God."

While it is true that any woman may come to Christ right where she is for salvation and to restore her broken relationship with God; it is also true that He will not leave her in her broken and sinful condition. It is His desire to transform us into His image and likeness. Being transformed into the image of God comes with a cost that can sometimes be quite exacting. Such changes may mean that our old traveling companions no longer like who we have become. Transformation may also require that we give up certain habits and diversions that were part of our old life. Being a citizen of God's kingdom will also require the total surrender of our citizenship within the kingdom of this world. To follow Christ as His ambassador will require becoming a foreigner in what was once your recognized home land.

"Therefore, "do not love the world or the things in the world. If anyone loves the world, the love of the Father is not in him. For all that is in the world – the lust of the flesh, the lust of the eyes, and the pride of life – is not of the Father but is of the world" (1 John 2:15-16). "Do you not know that friendship with the world is enmity with God? Whoever therefore wants to be a friend of the world makes himself an enemy of God" (James 4:4).

Perhaps rather than focusing on the cost of following Christ on this great adventure, we should focus on the reward. Any woman who follows Christ is gaining forgiveness for her sinful life, a new relationship with God as her Abba-Daddy, direct unencumbered access to the throne room of the God of the universe, and a divine eternal inheritance as the child of God. What price would someone be willing to pay for so great a reward? But wait there's more! The fearfully wonderful woman of God also gains unconditional love, unmerited acceptance, peace that passes all understanding and joy unspeakable and full of glory. She gains friendship with the friend (Jesus) who will never leave her or forsake her and who promises to stick close through thick and thin. Scripture tells us that it is in giving our lives away that we find life's greatest fulfillment and that it is the person who is willing to spend their life to the last blood drop who gains it back with blessing (Matthew 16:25-26). Who could ask for more?

If we are honest, those things that the disciple of Christ offers up freely for the glory of His kingdom are really nothing more than useless garbage when compared to the great richness of knowing Him and of being counted as his faithful companion and co-laborer (Philippians 3:7-9). What could possibly be of greater value than someone's eternal soul? What could hold more importance within our value system than having the security of an eternal home within a heavenly kingdom in the everlasting presence of our God and our King?

Christ reminds us that even though He is asking us to labor in his name and to take his yoke that his yoke will not be oppressive or too difficult. When we feel overburdened we can come to Him and find rest. We can take his assignments and carry our load even when that load needs to be pulled uphill because He is right beside us equipping us and providing the strength that we need (Matthew 11:28-30) . We can also be bold in sharing the good news of his salvation and in talking with others as ambassadors of his kingdom because he promises to provide us with the boldness, power and self-discipline required to represent him well to others (2 Timothy 1:7-8). If we carefully tally up the costs of following Jesus, they cannot possible compare to the blessings that he provides in exchange.

"And the ransomed of the LORD will return and come with joyful shouting to Zion, with everlasting joy upon their heads. They will find gladness and joy, and sorrow and sighing will flee away"- Isaiah 35:10

"He will wipe every tear from their eyes. There will be no more death or mourning or crying or pain, for the old order of things has passed away."- Revelation 21:4

GATHERING OUR LUGGAGE

As ambassadors for Christ, we might actually think of our temporary lives here on earth as a business trip. While we are here we have things to accomplish for the kingdom and things to learn about ourselves, our relationships with God and with others, and about our spiritual growth. Let's face it; such an important trip is going to require more than an overnight bag! Wouldn't it be great if we could gather up everything we wanted to take with us and simply pack it up? We want to be prepared. We may need a light sweater or a wrap on a chilly flight. Perhaps an easy reading book or magazine would be nice to have for any long delay at an airport. As ambassadors for Christ, we might actually think of our temporary lives here on earth as a business trip. While we are here we have things to accomplish for the kingdom in addition to things to learn about ourselves, our relationships with God and with others, and about our spiritual growth. Let's face it; such an important trip is going to require more than an overnight bag! Wouldn't it be great if we could simply gather up everything we wanted to take with us and pack it up? After all, we want to be prepared. We may need a light sweater or a wrap on a chilly flight. Perhaps an easy reading book or magazine would be nice to have for any long delay at an airport. A bottle of water and a few healthy snacks will keep us hydrated and prevent blood sugar levels from crashing. This could become vitally important in the fight against the fast food urge and the warm aromatic beckoning of cinnamon rolls while hurrying from gate to gate. The truth is that the less we carry the less we will have to worry over. It is sometimes amazing just how much we can live without and leave behind without really even missing it. To be wise packers, we will need to sort through everything as we go along. Much of what we may think is important now may actually prove to be excess baggage and in the end simply weigh us down.

Our preparation for the journey that lies ahead continues as we gather up our luggage pieces. Together we will lay out each piece and determine what we will need to pack in it.

We may find that some of these bags have been used for storage for things that we will no longer desire to carry on our trip. Hopefully, by looking at each luggage piece individually we will gather up the necessities for our journey and clean out the junk. Eliminating all the used up, worn out, musty and tired excess we've accumulated will give us ample room to pack properly for our trip. We've made our reservations, gathered our travel documents, planned our itinerary and collected our luggage. Before we start the actual packing, let's check on our flight status. Will we be traveling first class or coach? Surely none of us is willing to travel through life on stand-by!

※ ROADSIDE REFLECTIONS:

- What are the top ten criteria that you would use to select a traveling companion for a long journey?

- What does it mean to consider the costs? Have there been times that following Christ has cost you? Record how those times felt and how you responded to them in your travel journal.

✈

CHAPTER 3

What's Your Status?
Flying First Class never Coach

It is sadly true that many women find it more difficult to write down three things that they genuinely admire about themselves than to write down ten things that need improvement. Somehow, as women, we've gotten the message that to love ourselves is to be haughty or egotistical and arrogant. Perhaps this form of self-criticism has even become second nature for some of us. We probably rarely catch ourselves doing anything successfully or applaud ourselves for what we do well. Instead, the focus of our self -evaluation is usually on the negative or on our short-comings and what we may feel we lack when comparing ourselves to others. We may even feel silly or uncomfortable when others wait on us, notice us, or pay us a compliment.

Others of us may feel guilty for rewarding ourselves or for giving ourselves a special treat. For those of us in this category, guilt usually follows not long behind our having taken a break, put our feet up, or enjoyed our favorite chocolate candy, warm brownie or piece of cake. That guilt immediately shifts our focus back to the work we didn't complete or to those few extra pounds that we need to lose. We begin beating ourselves up for being lazy, unproductive or unattractive. We may even feel the need to hide our new purchases in the back of the closet or fib about how expensive that new dress was if we didn't catch it on a clearance rack.

Our self-talk has somehow convinced us that we are second class citizens undeserving of first class treatment or of spending full price.

⌘ ROADSIDE REFLECTIONS:

- Okay…If we're being honest (just us girls) do any of the descriptions used above sound at all like you? Ever? Even momentarily?

If we find ourselves being described in these first few paragraphs then we definitely are not traveling through life enjoying first-class accommodations. It may well be that we have become content to fly through life settling for coach or, worse yet, as a stand-by. Gals like us don't want to "make a fuss "and are happy just to somehow get a seat. Sadly, those of us counted among these women will never know the joy of sitting in the first-class section or of feeling lavished upon with life's finest pleasures. We have falsely convinced ourselves that we are unworthy and as such must be content in settling for whatever someone else is willing to offer us. Some may even fear rebuke or retaliation if she dare to ask for more or for better. Perhaps a few of us have accepted a form or counterfeit humility as a sign of true spirituality and have convinced ourselves that this faux faith form is what God requires of us.

How could so many of the world's wonderful women have come to devalue ourselves in such a way? From where do these feelings of self-loathing, insecurity or inferiority that many of us carry originate? What fuels the widely accepted attitude that being female is somehow being second best? We will begin our search for answers to these questions by examining the incorrect religious, political and philosophical teachings about what it means to be a woman that influence our thinking.

False religious teachings contribute to the concept that because women are created in a secondary status by God they are of lesser value and therefore deserving of lesser consideration, representation and protection under the law. These messages of inferiority or secondary status are subtle yet wide spread. Most of us begin receiving these messages in infancy. Everywhere around us we receive cultural messages that subliminally signal that girls are secondary, less desired, weaker, and otherwise don't quite measure up to boys. We hear it from late night humor, from music lyrics, from common phrases such as: "You throw like a girl" or "stop crying like a girl". Most sadly, we hear it from the pulpits and lecterns of churches, temples and Synagogues. Scripture and holy text is often incorrectly used to substantiate these messages of female subservience. The end result for many females is the adoption of a negative attitude towards God and a feeling of hopelessness. How can we possibly believe that we have a Father God who loves us while enduring unjust and oppressive treatment simply because of our sex? Many women have come to believe that if there is a God at all He certainly must not care.

Yet, if we examine the scriptures, beginning with the Old Testament, we find that the God of the Jewish and Christian faith does care about women. He communed with women openly and directly, and had great concern for their difficult life situations. For example, in Genesis chapter sixteen (16) we find the story of the slave woman Hagar and read that she communed with God in the wilderness after fleeing harsh treatment at the hands of her mistress. She is amazed that this God, who is the God of the Jews and not the God of her original people group, has taken notice of her plight with compassion. In her conversation with God, Hagar gives this God who was previously unknown to her a name and refers to Him as "*EL Roi*". This name has been translated as "the God who sees me."(Zodhiates, S.T. (1994). Scripture teaches us in Hebrews 13:8 that God is forever the same. If this is true, then it follows that the very same God that took notice of a run- away slave girl and had compassion upon Hagar still takes notice and moves with compassion at the oppression, abuse and harsh treatment of women across the globe today. God still sees hopeless and distressed women and He still cares.

✵ ROADSIDE REFLECTIONS:

- How does it make you feel to know that "the God above all other gods" sees and knows you in your daily struggles and distress?

In various cultures across our globe women face incredible challenges and hardships simply because they are born non-male. These religious and political teachings that support the notion that women are inferior human beings or second rate citizens in the eyes of God have been used for centuries and within many nations and religious ideologies as justification for brutality, oppression, rape, female infanticide, and most recently for sex selection abortion. This latest practice is completely legal within the United States and is growing in popularity globally. Surprisingly, the practice of determining the sex of an unborn child and then aborting that child if the sex is not as desired hasn't received much social stigma or negative cultural response. Proponents of population control see this practice as a viable and practical alternative to population over-growth in impoverished countries as well as to the birth of undesired children. The tests to determine the sex of an unborn fetus which precede a sex-selection abortion are relatively inexpensive ($300) with over 1400 different types being sold directly to the consumer to be used in the privacy of their homes.

In an article published by LifeStyle News in December of 2006, the United Nations reported that the poor country of India has the greatest use of sex-selection abortion. Based upon these United Nations' findings, as many as 7000 girls are killed by abortion every day in that nation. The report, issued in 2006, goes on to claim that dramatic declines in the number of girls being born within the most prosperous districts of this nation have been documented since 1991. As many as 50-100 fewer girls per 1,000 boys are being found in these regions compared to elsewhere. The United Nations attributes these statistics to the devaluation of women, the costs of marrying off a daughter, and to the increased accessibility of sex-selection abortion.

Proponents of radical feminist theories have justifiably taken offense to false teachings, harsh treatments and oppressive ideologies such as those mentioned above. The arguments and suppositions being offered by these theorists have also failed to offer a correct perspective or a proper solution to the plight of women. Sadly, the larger portion of feminist philosophies has failed women and has deceived women by convincing them to exchange the truth of God's design for females for yet another lie. Under these radical feminist ideologies, women have been encouraged to see men as their oppressors and are taught that in order to secure a desired position of equal status with their male counterparts they must abandon their feminine ways of thinking, looking and responding due to their inferiority to male mannerisms. The basic argument is that if a woman is to compete in a "man's" world then she must begin to think and to act more like men. A more androgynous or blended display of characteristics and behaviors is preferred under this approach with the softer, gentler and more nurturing behaviors generally identified as feminine being discouraged as the product of sexist cultural conditioning and their adoption as a sign of weakness. Women are cautioned that nice girls finish last and that being soft will not produce the desired outcome or achievement. Such teaching, while offering women empowerment and the hope of equality and respect, is often still unbalanced, one sided and rooted in lies.

The first lie impacting our choice in flight status is found contained within the supposition that males are our enemies with whom we must struggle or compete against in the age old "battle of the sexes". If we examine God's divine purpose for creating both the male and the female we quickly learn that males are neither our enemies nor our competition. Rather than to compete, it was God's desire for the male and the female to complement and to complete one another. His design for the two parts of his created biological pair was that in the uniting of the two distinct, uniquely different parts there would be the completion of one flesh and of one being. It is only in the uniting of the two distinct sets of complementary characteristics and responses that the total expression of all of God's attributes is possible.

Each of the biological sexes is created in God's image and bears His likeness in character and in mannerism or response. Males and females are distinct physically, emotionally and spiritually by design. Neither sex is superior nor is either sex inferior. Males display certain of God's attributes while females display others. When the two parts work together, as God intended, then the total of the Godhead and all of God's character is displayed and enacted. God intended a perfect unity of the pair. Contrary to the teachings of the feminist theorists and philosophers, females must embrace their feminine ways of knowing and doing as being God- given and as bearing His likeness and attributes of His character. To express a feminine character is not to express inferiority or weakness any more than to express a male character is to express superiority. The characteristics of both sexes must be freely expressed the total Godhead to be visible within human interactions and for all the attributes of God to be displayed.

GOD IS A SPIRIT AND UNLIKE ANY MAN

Commonly recited scriptural text and holy writing most often refer to the being of God in male gendered pronouns and as occupying male dominated social positions or performing male roles such as those of father, judge, ruler or King. This use of male gendering in describing the Godhead can leave women who have had a problem with abuse at the hands of human males with a skewed picture of their creator and sovereign. Consider that if a woman has an earthly father who is distant, absent or abusive then she may transfer the negative characteristics of her earthly father to her idea or concept of God. Such transference may result in having difficulty relating to a "Heavenly Father" in a positive manner or in seeing this being as loving, trustworthy or caring. The good news for such women is that in actuality God has no gender identity and bears no physical sexual characteristics. Scripture tells us that God is a spirit (Isaiah 31:3, Daniel 4:9, John 4:24). While it is true that God took on a male physical form in the person of Jesus Christ when we desired for us to identify with him as our High Priest and Savior; as a spiritual being, God is not strictly confined strictly to masculine or feminine character traits nor is he housed in a physical form (Luke 24:39). Scripture also teaches us that God is the complete godhead and therefore he lacks nothing. In God all things are contained and are complete (Colossians 1: 16-17). As a complete being God would contain and display all possible characteristics and attributes. The conclusion of these scriptures would be that God is a spirit that is not limited to male characteristics or to female characteristics. As a complete being, He is fully male and fully female.

An example for God possessing and displaying what we would categorize as both male and female characteristics can be found in one of the names that the God of the Israelites uses to express His character and His care for His chosen people. That name is "*El-Shaddai*" (Genesis 17:1, 28:3, 35:11). The prefix "*El*" is used within the Hebrew language to refer to a being that is all powerful or almighty. The name "*Shaddai*" (sometimes printed "*shad day*") is derived from another word, "*shad*", which means breast in the Hebrew (Zodhiates, 1994). In using this name, God is comparing His nurturing care for His people to that of someone with breasts suckling an infant.

The image that the God above all gods conveys to Father Abraham contains all the attributes of a loving mother, who nourishes, comforts and completely satisfies the infant at her breast. *El Shaddai* is the source of all that His children need and He will freely give it to them.

God first used this name, *El Shaddai*, when speaking with the patriarch Abraham while instituting the covenant of circumcision; which was the practice of removing the foreskin from the penis of all males born within His chosen tribes of people. It is God as "*El*" who helps His people with His mighty, all abundant power, but it is God as "*Shaddai*" who blesses and supplies all His children's needs by freely giving of himself. If having the qualities of being nurturing and caring toward children, which are typically assigned as feminine gender traits, were deemed inferior then certainly God would not have ascribed those qualities to Himself.

It is also important to note that the prefix "*El*" or "*all powerful*" is used before the name "*Shaddai*". Combining the two names in such a manner identifies one who has breasts and who is nurturing and gives of themself freely as also being powerful and mighty. Being mighty and powerful does not have to be in contradiction or opposition to being nurturing and giving. The two seemingly dichotomous characteristics can exist within the same being. One can be powerful and mighty and still be nurturing and concerned about the welfare of others. Jesus wept over the grief displayed by Mary and Martha at the death of their brother Lazarus. He also stooped down in total humility to take up a servant's wash bowl and wash the dirty feet of his disciples. He had a tender heart and a compassionate spirit and yet was the manliest man that ever lived.

ROADSIDE REFLECTIONS:

- Were you a "Daddy's girl" growing up? What does it mean to you as a fearfully wonderful woman of God to be a spiritual "Daddy's girl" after reading the above paragraphs that introduce us to God as "El Shaddai"?

If we, as fearfully wonderful women, follow the precepts of radical feminism and exchange our feminine ways of interacting and responding to the needs of others to adopt exclusively male mannerisms and ways of interaction then we eliminate those aspects of God's character which He chose to display through females. Those attributes of God will be removed from our human interaction, our spiritual life, and our earthly existence. The result will be an incomplete, unbalanced picture of God and a tragic loss to our human cultures.

This book is written to those women who are in relationship with Christ and profess to be Christians. We will continue our search for answers by examining the teachings of Christianity as they relate to the status of women. The foundational basis for Christianity is the teachings and earthly examples that Jesus gave while living on the earth, so we will begin our search with him. Christ's life and ministry is recorded within the New Testament books of the Bible beginning with the gospels. Searching through these texts will reveal that Jesus' teachings and behavior often contradicted the social norms of his culture regarding the status and treatment of women. We will find that just like His Heavenly Father, Jesus openly interacted with women. He also talked about women, used women as illustrations and positive role models, and included women in his ministry and teaching. Women were included within the community of disciples who followed him.

As followers of Christ, we must remember that we are called to be "in the world" but not "of the world" (John 15:19). Our perspective on the status and treatment of women must be based upon God's principles and instructions rather than on man-made religious systems or political agendas. We will discover as followers of Christ that just like our leader we will need to stand in opposition to all teachings and ideologies that oppress and subjugate women. Women in the kingdom of Christ always fly first class! We are the daughters and royal ambassadors of the King of Kings and The God above all gods. It is our relationship to Him that establishes our first class status. He created us with perfect purpose and perfect design.

✳ ROADSIDE REFLECTIONS:

- As we travel this earth as an Ambassador of God, we will come across difficult people and paths or treacherous territory and rocky terrain. In such circumstances, which Characteristic or aspect of God do you find the most important or most comforting/faith reinforcing? We have already discussed a few names of God that we can call upon as we travel along. What other characteristics/attributes of God are most important for you as you travel along your life journey?

ESTABLISHING FIRST CLASS STATUS

It doesn't take a degree in rocket science to determine that men and women are different. The issue of debate among psychologists, sociologists and theologians is regarding how much of that difference can be attributed to genetic make-up or biology and how much is directly related to cultural influences, definitions of gender roles, and a person's upbringing. The recognition of differences between the sexes eventually brings up the question of whether or not one of the sexes is the preferred, dominant or "more correct"; thus leaving the other sex of secondary or less preferred status. The answer to this question becomes the dividing line between varying political, social and religious ideologies and positions.

Scripture will demonstrate that while it is true that God created the male and the female with very distinct giftings, characteristics and attributes; both sexes reflect his character and bear his stamp of approval. Both the male and the female have distinct functions and purpose within God's divine order. We will begin our search for truth regarding these questions at the beginning. The following scriptures are from the first book of the Bible and are taken from the creation accounts. These four verses examine God's creation of the female and contain how He describes her as well as her relationship to the man and to her God.

"So God created man in his own image, in the image of God he created him; male and female he created them. God blessed them and said to them, "Be fruitful and increase in number; fill the earth and subdue it. Rule over the fish of the sea and the birds of the air and over every living creature that moves on the ground." -Genesis 1:27-28

"The LORD God said, "It is not good for the man to be alone. I will make a helper suitable for him."-Genesis 2:18

"The man said, this is now bone of my bones and flesh of my flesh; she shall be called woman, for she was taken out of man." For this reason a man will leave his father and mother and be united to his wife and they will become one flesh"-Genesis 2:23-24.

"When God created man, he made him in the likeness of God. He created them male and female and blessed them. And when they were created, he called them man.-Genesis 5:1-2

THE ORIGINS OF SECONDARY STATUS LIE #1: PUTTING WORDS IN GOD'S MOUTH.

The first group of false religious teachings supporting the secondary status of women finds its basis in the argument that females were created in secondary status to males. That is to say, that the secondary status of females is the intended order of God from her creation. This group of teachings goes on to suggest that the creation of females was an afterthought or of secondary importance to that of the creation of the male. However, if we examine the creation scriptures taken from the book of Genesis and printed above do not find any indication that the female in God's creation was any less blessed or of any less importance to Him. As a matter of fact, the scripture found in Genesis 2:18 suggests that God had a specific purpose in creating the female exactly when and as He did. Not one of the accounts of the creation of man and woman contained within these passages in Genesis supports the supposition that females are, by God's design, of secondary importance or status. These scriptures indicate that God created both the male and the female of the species in His image. God did not merely give the male His image and His character. Both the male and the female bear the image of God and both are to be respected and honored as both bear His likeness and his attributes. The male and the female may reflect different attributes and display different characteristics of their creator but each sex uniquely displays facets of God's image none the less.

This first group of false teachings further suggests that only males are created with inherent right to dominion over the earth. Again, an examination of the scriptural text contained in Genesis contradicts these claims. In the scripture found in Genesis 1:27-28, God commands *both sexes* to be fruitful and to subdue the earth. Both the male and the female were included in God's declaration of their dominance and responsibility for His creation. While it is true that Adam's response and interaction to his environment is different to that of Eve's response and it is also true that they displayed their responsibility and dominion in distinct manner; nowhere in the scriptural accounts of creation does God verbalize any subordination of the female or His preference for the male. Nowhere does God exclude the female from the responsibility for the care and dominion of His beloved creation. Both the male and female were given the mandate to be caretakers and both followed that mandate utilizing their God-given attributes and characteristics. Adam initiated. He busily went about naming his animals and establishing structure, order and control. Eve responded. She went about communicating; connecting and seeking to understand how every aspect of her surroundings were inter-related to herself and to each other. Adam directed while Eve nurtured. Eve questioned and communicated while Adam ordered and dictated. Each of the sexes' responses to their environment and their manner of assuming dominion is the direct product of their divine design and created purpose in God's order of things.

THE ORIGINS OF SECONDARY STATUS LIE #2: PUTTING THINGS IN NATURAL ORDER

Another group of false teachings defends its argument for the secondary status of women by focusing simplistically on the chronological order of creation. This group suggests that because the male was created first he has the greater importance. The false logic of this thinking should be quite apparent. Basing importance or status of a created thing simply on the chronological order of appearance within the creation account would suggest that dry land and oceans, created on day three, are of greater significance than the sun and the moon because they did not appear until day four. Of course, then the Sun and the moon would have greater importance than sea life and birds as these did not come into being until day five. Following this chain of flawed logic to its conclusion, we would have to concede that all of the above mentioned components of His creation are of greater importance to God than His most beloved creation which He called "man". This could be the only possible conclusion using the logic of chronology given that God did not place humans on the earth until day six. How ridiculous! Would it be better logic to conclude that God placed each aspect of His creation into being at precisely the correct time? It would have been foolish to place human beings into an environment that lacked proper light, water, atmosphere, food bearing vegetation and other elements essential to survival and healthy existence. Interestingly enough, some ecologically based pagan ideologies have taken this flawed logic as the basis of their theology and do suggest that humans are of less importance than the earth and the sky and that the life of a tree has more value than that of a human fetus.

It is important when considering such ideologies as those above to remember that God told the man and the woman to take control and responsibility for His creation (Genesis 1:27-28). This was their assigned role and not one that humans assumed unlawfully. A clear distinction must also be made between humans and all other living creatures as humans are the only members of God's creation made in His image and endowed with His character. Certainly, any life form that God made in His own image and likeness is of greater value than one that does not bear His image. Scripture supports the ideology that humans of both sexes are created by God with a higher status than all other life forms and have the rightful responsibility for domination over God's creation. This is the intended natural order of God's plan.

THE ORIGINS OF SECONDARY STATUS LIE #3: PROVIDING MAN
A LITTLE HELP

Still other teachings touting the secondary status of women rely upon an improper interpretation of the word "helper" or "helpmate" to support their stance. In Genesis 2:18 God describes His purpose in creating woman as that of providing man with a *"suitable helper"*. This third group of false teachings has defined woman's created status of *"helper"* as that of being a servant or a hireling and therefore of a secondary, subservient position to the man. The claim of this group of teachings is that God created woman with the intended purpose of being a servant to man and not as that of his equal or partner. Practitioners following this religious ideology will not allow women to "rule over" men by teaching them, governing them or taking any position of authority over them.

According to Biblical scholars, the Hebrew word used to describe the status of woman at the point of creation in Genesis 2:18 is `*ezer* (Zodhiates, 1994*)*. This identical word (`*ezer*) is used several times within the scriptures in reference to God Himself. A few such examples can be found within the Psalms. In Psalms 33:20, the psalmist refers to God as our "help" and our shield and again in Psalms 70:5, God is the "help" and the deliverer of a poor and needy psalmist. Psalm115:9-11 refers to God as the "help and the shield" of Israel and the House of Aaron three separate times. Are we to assume that when the Psalmist used the same identical word "`*ezer*" within each of these referenced scriptures to describe a function of God He meant for God to be portrayed as subservient or of a secondary status? What man is there who can control or command Yahweh (Lamentations 3:37)? Would any man dare to suggest that God is of a secondary status to his created being? Such a thought would be blasphemy. There must be a better interpretation or understanding for this word .

Zodhiates' lexicon of the Hebrew and Chaldee language translates the word used in the account of the creation of woman to mean *"helpmate, aid and companion"* (Zodhiates, S.T. (1994). If this same word is used to reference Almighty God, then it becomes quite clear that to be a helper or a companion (`*ezer*) cannot denote a secondary or subservient status given that Yahweh rules above everything and everyone. A helpmate or companion is not the equivalent of a servant or the hired help if God can be described as serving in this position. Eve was created as Adam's helpmate. As such she was designed to respond to Adam's physical, emotional , psychological and spiritual needs. She was to interpret those needs and then to provide companionship, additional strength and greater insight as Adam's situation required. She was to come along side and make up the lacking difference. Adam initiated and Eve responded and often Eve saw a need and initiated a response before Adam even knew what his exact need was.

An interesting point to be made regarding the creation of the woman is what God deduced that lead him to decide to create her in the first place. Why was woman created? Why was her presence within the garden necessary? Based upon the scripture in Genesis 2:18, God concluded that the male of His creation was incomplete, lonely and lacking something when he was functioning on his own. God concluded upon seeing the man alone that the situation was "not good". To correct the situation God created the woman. The creation of the female was the improvement to a "not good" situation in God's eyes. She was not an afterthought but rather God's solution or help to the unfinished condition of a man being alone. She was man's *ezer*: his help.

THE ORIGINS OF SECONDARY STATUS LIE #4: PROVIDING WOMAN THE NECESSARY PROTECTION

The final group of false teachings that we will examine suggests that women are more easily deceived or more susceptible to the control of evil influences than men; therefore they are spiritually weaker. The basis for this set of teachings is rooted in the idea that it was Eve who sinned first and Eve who caused the man, Adam, to sin. This teaching concludes that it was the woman who caused the man to fall and who brought sin's devastation upon all of creation. According to this ideology, sin entered the earth because the woman was more easily beguiled by the serpent's lies and had more interaction or conversation with him. The conclusion is that perhaps man would not have sinned if woman had not manipulated or beguiled him and women are therefore not to be trusted.

This religious ideology demands that all women be placed under "the covering" or supervising authority of a man for both the man's and the woman's spiritual protection as well as for the supervision of the gullible woman. According to this mindset, because it was the first woman, Eve, who was deceived by Satan; all women must now be spiritually policed and controlled. Women are seen as the weaker spiritual vessel. This religious ideology when carried to its most extreme form is still used to support wife beating and stoning within many fundamentalist, zealot groups.

In Genesis Chapter 2, we read that human beings had one created responsibility: to care for the garden (Genesis 2:15), and one direct prohibition: not to eat from the tree of the knowledge of good and evil (Genesis 2:17). We have previously established that the man and the woman are created distinctly different and as such interact with and respond to their environment differently. Regardless of their created uniqueness, it is important to point out that both Adam and Eve each individually had the same choice. They could individually choose to either obey God or to break His only commandment and eat from that tree. Each operated under the same God- given free will and God-given mandate. There was no confusion; each knew the consequence of choosing disobedience because God outlined His terms for them in Genesis 2:17. Both Adam and Eve individually chose willful, deliberate rejection of God's command and intentional disobedience with the full knowledge of what God had told them would happen (Genesis 3:6). While it is true that their reactions were different; the consequence of their individual decisions was the fall of all of creation and the complete alteration of humankind's relationship with God forevermore (Genesis 3:6-24).

Eve interacted and communicated with the serpent. She responded to her interaction with doubt of God's instruction and chose to disobey his command. Adam, however, was not helpless against the woman Eve. He had the working knowledge of God's law and a personal relationship with his creator. Adam could have refused the fruit from Eve, called her into repentance, called upon his God for forgiveness and consequently changed the whole situation. He did not. Both parties chose to sin. Their sin may have been displayed differently but at the foundational level both the man and the woman knowingly disobeyed God's instruction.

At the exact moment that each of them took a bite of that forbidden fruit, both Adam and Eve were instantaneously aware of their personal sin and of their corporate fallen condition (Genesis 3:7). They immediately made coverings for their nakedness and then hid themselves away when they heard their God coming (Genesis 3:8). Why? Hadn't the man and woman been naked from the beginning? Didn't God create each of them in a state of nakedness when He placed them within His garden? Who instructed the man and the woman of a need for clothing? Who shamed them into hiding away when they had walked previously in their nakedness out in the open?

It is important to note that neither Adam nor Eve chose to cry out to God or to run to their loving creator for forgiveness or help. Both chose to make their own covering for their sin and to hide their shame. What were they trying to accomplish by their actions? Did they suppose that God would not notice? This prideful act of trying to hide their shame and devise their own remedy was sin heaped upon their original sin. Adam and Eve tried to hide their sin from God after they committed it. They tried to cover it up with a self-made remedy. How might the outcome have been different if the first humans had responded to their disobedience in repentance or sought forgiveness?

This first act of sin not only forever changed the relationship between God and his creation but also altered the relationship between the first man and the woman that God had created especially for him and then presented to him. While God's intended purpose in the creation of this first couple was for them to be lifetime partners in the caretaking of God's creation; sin caused each of the partners to act in a total individualistic and selfish manner. God desired perfect unity for the couple while sin caused a division between the man and the woman. The woman was God's solution for the man's loneliness and need. She was the only other being on the planet who was Adam's suitable companion and mate and yet the now sinful Adam quickly shifted focus and blame to Eve when he was caught in sin.

In Genesis 3:12 after Adam is found guilty of disobedience, we see him try to shift blame for his sin to the woman. God asked him if he had eaten of the forbidden tree and Adam tried to get the focus off of himself by stating that it was Eve who brought the fruit to him *and then* he ate it. How quickly Adam changed from extolling Eve as "bone of my bone and flesh of my flesh" in Genesis 2:23 to now referring to his partner rather impersonally as "the woman that thou gavest to be with me". If it is true that God did in fact give Eve to Adam then didn't he bear responsibility to care for her and to protect her under God's mandate to care for all of his creation? Was Eve not included as a part of that creation? Carefully notice that God didn't react to Adam's blame shifting then and he still doesn't respond to it today. If we read the outline of God's judgment for sin beginning in Genesis 3:14 we see that God held all three of the offenders responsible and passed separate and distinct judgments on all three guilty parties. He passed judgment upon the serpent first, then upon the woman, then upon the man, and finally upon all vegetation of the ground (Genesis 3:14-20).

Also note that nowhere in God's decree to the woman or to the man does He state that the woman is more responsible for the entrance of sin and the consequential fall of all of His creation. In Genesis 3:17, God tells Adam that the ground is cursed because of his sin. He does not discuss the repercussions of Eve's sin with Adam or direct responsibility for her sin to him. Eve bore that responsibility all for herself.

Eve was not spiritually naïve or ignorant. In Genesis 3:2-3 she clearly understood God's commands and was able to quote his instructions back to the serpent. She did embroider upon God's precise instructions when reciting them as God never told the man or the woman that they could not even *touch* the tree as Eve stated (Genesis 3:3). Even though Eve tried to blame the serpent for her disobedience God knew that she was not manipulated out of her ignorance (Genesis 3:13). Eve had direct access and interaction with her creator. She could have gone to her husband or to God at any time to discuss her conversation with the serpent and her resulting confusion. She willfully chose to rebel against God's explicit instructions and, using her own reasoning, came to the conclusion that God would doubtfully keep His word (Genesis 3:6). Eve also abandoned her divine design and created purpose. She failed to act as the loving partner, trusted companion and as part of a single unit (couple). God had designed her to be with Adam. Eve knew she was in serious breach of God's law the moment she ate that fruit (Genesis 3:6-7). She could have repented on the spot and kept her husband out of the resulting situation. Instead, she chose to include Adam in her transgression. While Adam's sin caused him to blame Eve; Eve failed to ask for mercy for her husband or to come to his defense. She obviously wasn't a good advisor either as she didn't encourage Adam to repent or to call upon God when she realized that they were both fallen. Eve failed Adam as his helpmate. Sin caused the man and the woman to distance themselves from each other, from their God, and from their divine created purpose and function. No intimate human relationship would ever be the same again. Eve was held accountable by God for her sinful disobedience. Judgment was handed down against her and against every female relative to come as a consequence (Genesis 3:15-16).

✠ ROADSIDE REFLECTIONS:

- This reading has been a long one and it relates to the most controversial and widely accepted of all the false teachings regarding women. After reading this section what are your comments, thoughts or questions?

- Would do you define the word 'Ezer' differently after this reading?

- How do you feel about the idea of women being more susceptible to spiritual deceit and sin and therefore needing a "covering" or an authority?

- Do you feel differently about the role of women in the church or about yourself?

IN THE MIDST, GOD HAD A PERFECT PLAN

Contained within this passage of scripture in Genesis chapter 3, and significantly recorded prior to God's judgment decree upon the woman and the man, is the greatest of God's promises. Genesis chapter 3verse fifteen (3:15) contains the first recording of the promise of the coming Messiah, Jesus. In this scripture, He is referred to as the "seed of the woman".

God is speaking directly to the serpent in verse fifteen (3:15) when He foretells of the enmity between the two beings that would follow. God declares to the serpent that the "seed of the woman" is going to bruise the serpent's head. The redemption for mankind's sin and the restitution price for their disobedience would be delivered by the "seed of a woman". How loving of God to declare the solution for mankind's sinful and fallen status before actually passing judgment upon them (Genesis 3:16-19)

God, in the form of Jesus, would come to earth to live in the flesh. He would be born in human form but unlike any other because his origin would be from a virgin's birth. The virgin birth of the Messiah is a highly significant point because the Messiah had to be sinless and could not be charged guilty under God's judgment of original sin (Genesis 3:16-19) All blood ancestors of Adam would be born under this judgment (Romans 5:12). Just as Eve was taken directly out of Adam without an earthly father or the need for human sperm; the Messiah would be taken from a woman without the need for a biological father or the use of human sperm. He would be "seed of a woman" without being seed of a man.

Jesus' sinlessness could only be accomplished if he were truly God incarnate and yet completely without personal sin or being found guilty under law due to inherited original sin. While the false religious teachings of human men may not trust women with spiritual discernment or leadership, God chose a woman to fulfill His greatest plan. God chose to use the woman, Mary, as the vehicle to bring the gift of His son to the world. He could have just miraculously caused Jesus to appear. He could have created him from the dust of the earth as He did Adam. He could have taken Him from Mary's body without a conception and a birth. None of those origins would have fulfilled the requirement that the Messiah be "seed of woman" and totally human yet without sin (Hebrews 4:15-16).

God chose a completely unique manner in which to deliver His greatest gift to mankind.

While Eve was willing to reason with the serpent and to explicitly disobey God's command; Mary heard the voice of God and was willing to cooperate in full obedience to God's plan (Luke 1:38). Through Eve's disobedience and willing sin God passed judgment on all mankind but Mary's obedience and willing submission ushered in God's salvation and grace to all humanity. God would not have chosen a woman, a descendent of Eve, to fulfill his plan of salvation if, as these false religions suggest, all of the female creation is not to be trusted in spiritual matters. Likewise an examination of the scripture recounting Gabriel's announcement of God's plan to Mary does not indicate that God or his messenger spoke with a man who was appointed as Mary's "spiritual authority" or "covering" prior to speaking with her (Luke 1:26-38).The angel spoke directly to the unmarried woman while she was alone. While the religious paradigms of some men may not trust women in spiritual matters; God clearly does.

Praise God that it was the "seed of a woman" who came to earth to redeem and to elevate the status of all women forevermore. If, according to false teachings on spiritual covering, Eve's sin and willingness to listen to and then obey the serpent forfeited man's ability to trust women in spiritual matters then shouldn't Mary's sensitivity to the Holy Spirit and willingness to obey the voice of God redeem back women's trustworthiness and spiritual reliability at least to some degree?

Women were never second rate creations within God's plan. We are trusted helpmates, companions, partners with full authority, and the spiritual daughters of God. We will further learn that the examples of Jesus and the teachings of the New Testament have elevated women to the status of joint heirs, co-laborers, ambassadors and members of the Royal Priesthood of believers. That makes us very important people in God's heavenly kingdom. When we travel with Jesus we travel V.I.P.

CHAPTER 4

Daring to Travel V.I.P.

CHOOSING YOUR CABIN AND SEAT

Each woman who chooses to follow Christ must decide for herself what she knows to be true regarding the value of women, her personal calling and giftings, and her position within the authority structure of her home church as well as within the Body of Christ. Knowing who she is in Christ Jesus and establishing her value to the kingdom of God are foundational to her ability to stand against the lies and half-truths that religion, culture and her enemy will hurl at her. These lies and half-truths will cripple and bind her and keep her from completing her assigned duties as an ambassador to God's kingdom if she doesn't know how to combat their effects with truth. Remember, it is the truth that sets us free (John 8:32). Choosing to travel V.I.P. is the decision to recognize and to affirm that you are a very important person in the Kingdom of God. Such a decision can best be made by getting alone with God and listening for His voice and His leading. Understanding what the scripture truly says outside of denominational teaching and tradition will be vital. It is only when we know Our Creator intimately and allow Him to reveal His truth to us that we have a sure understanding of who we are.

Traveling with Jesus

Jesus never personally gave any specific instructions or teachings outlining the role of women within the early church. He did not leave any particular guidance pertaining to the specific treatment of women within the home or the community. Most of the Biblical instructions cited today pertaining to church order, the positions or authority that women may hold, and the roles that women may perform within the church are drawn from the teachings of the Apostle Paul as recorded in his letters to the early church. To understand the position Jesus took regarding women and ministry we must examine his habits, routines and interactions with women during his earthly life. Upon doing so, it will become quite apparent that his attitude toward women was very different from what was customary for the culture in which he lived.

For example, Jewish women of that historical time period were generally not well educated and received most of their teaching from their parents (Cargal, Timothy B. (1997). They were not taught by Rabbis and did not attend religious schools or receive synagogue instruction as did the young boys. Unlike other Rabbis of his time, Jesus considered women worthy of spiritual instruction. Luke 10:38-42 records the story of the two sisters of Lazarus, Mary and Martha. Martha assumed all the customary duties of a good Jewish woman. She was responsible for the household and was busy cleaning, cooking and caring for her guest. Her sister, Mary, broke with convention and sat at Jesus' feet to receive direct instructions similar to the action of any of his disciples. Jesus taught Mary face to face and encouraged her sister, Martha, to come sit down and be taught by him as well.

The focus for the role of a "good" Jewish woman was centered on domestic activities such as birthing and raising children, and the care of the home. (Ward, Kaari (1987). Due to strict moral codes, unmarried women lived within their parents' household and women did not travel great distances unaccompanied (Corley, Kathleen (1993). Scripture clearly identifies women as traveling with Jesus along with his disciples (Luke 8:1-3). Some of the names of women listed within the scripture among those who traveled with Jesus include: Mary Magdalene, Joanna, Mary the mother of James and Joseph, and Susanna. Recall also that it was his female followers who chose to remain to be with Jesus at his crucifixion after all his male apostles with the exception of John the Beloved had fled in fear of losing their own lives (Matthew 27:55-56). These women traveled with Jesus and his disciples for a greater purpose than merely conforming to stereotypical female roles such as caring for the men and preparing meals. They were actively involved in his ministry.

As was custom, it was the women who would come to care for his body at the tomb and therefore were the first to hear the good news of his resurrection (Matthew 28: 5-10). Scripture tells us that Jesus spoke to Mary in the garden of the tomb and then told her to go share the news with the brethren (John 20:1-18).This action is highly significant as custom often excluded the testimony of a woman as being permissible in a court of law. It is also exhilarating and freeing as we realize that Jesus appointed a woman to go share his very important news with the male followers. The first missionary of the gospel appointed by the resurrected Jesus himself was a woman. Jesus trusted a woman to deliver the greatest story ever told to his waiting disciples. Hallelujah!

Jesus also used women as positive illustrations when teaching kingdom principles in his parables. While it may be true that only a select few of his parables include women, it is significant that He included them at all. We must remember the patriarchal or male dominant structure of the culture in which he was teaching, and the clear distinction between public (male) and private (female) spheres of domain to which they adhered. We can infer from Jesus' use of women as examples or principal characters that he considered the characteristics or attributes customarily ascribed to women to be worthy as examples for men to follow. These feminine roles of being nurturing, caring, giving healers were chosen by Jesus to portray God's kingdom and suggested as desirable traits to be developed within male followers of Christ. We can also postulate that perhaps Jesus was trying to connect with the women in his audience by using examples with whom they could relate. A list of a few of Jesus' parables that took illustrations from women's lives or pointed to a woman's admirable actions would include: The woman mixing yeast into dough (Mathew 12:33), The ten virgins (Matthew 25:1-13), The woman with the lost coin (Luke 15:8-10), The widow who gave all that she had (Luke 21:1-4) and The widow who persistently sought justice (Luke 18:1-8).

Jesus' compassionate interaction with women was not reserved for the women who followed his teachings or even limited to women who were upright members of the Jewish community. Scripture cites several examples of his interactions with non-Jewish women as well as with women who were of poor social standing or fallen reputation. One such example is his interaction with a Greek woman from the region of Syrian Phoenicia who had a demon possessed daughter (Mark 7:26). Many scholars suggest that this woman was probably the member of a wealthy social group based upon the fact that her daughter lay on a bed rather than on a mat (Mark 7:30). Based upon scripture, it is clear that she is not a recognized follower of Jesus' teachings or a Jewess as He tells her it is incorrect to give to her by taking away from His children (Mark 7: 27). She was clearly an outsider and had no claim to his favor or right to demand his attention yet she continued to call out to Jesus for mercy on her daughter's behalf. Jesus praised this woman for her persistent faith and delivered her daughter from her torment immediately (Mark 7:25-30).

In another situation Jesus interacted respectfully with a Samaritan woman who had come down to her town well alone to draw water. Good, upright Jews did not speak to Samaritans. The cultural distain between these two groups was very widespread and evident. Jesus even used this hatred as an illustration in his parable of The Good Samaritan (Luke 10:25-37). No Jewish Rabbi would have been seen publicly speaking to a Samaritan woman and would have particularly shunned this one as she had a tarnished reputation even among her own people for living with men that she had not married. Yet Jesus spoke freely and openly with this woman, forgave her of her sins which he recalled to her in detail, and offered her salvation and eternal life (John 4:4-4239-42).

The final example taken from Jesus' earthly life to which we will call attention is one that illustrates his value of women as individuals deserving of his love and attention. This particular event occurred shortly before his arrest and subsequent crucifixion. Luke 7:36-50 records the story of a woman with a sketchy moral past who burst into a dinner party and disrupted the host's schedule to anoint Jesus' feet with a pricey perfume oil . She continued her spectacle by mopping up the mess she had made with her hair. Jesus was the invited dinner guest of a Pharisee residing within that town. The sinful past and degraded reputation of the woman who made the spectacle of herself as she anointed Jesus' feet was common knowledge among those in attendance. As she continued her show, the dinner host wanted to throw her out in disgrace and the disciples grumbled about her wasteful disregard for the expense of her irresponsible actions. Jesus, however, praised this woman for her act of total devotion and abandon as well as for her faith. He told her that her faith "had saved her" (Luke 7:50). Jesus did not succumb to religious pressures or to the tradition of male superiority over women in this scenario. He was not offended that a sinful woman openly displayed her worship and adoration of him in such a public manner. He chose to praise this sinful woman in the presence of all the self-righteous town folks and pious Pharisees in attendance who had so harshly judged her.

The actions of Jesus such as those listed above clearly broke with social norms and cultural attitudes regarding women. Christ's teaching and interactions with others often challenged the social conventions, religious ideologies and customs of his time. His words and actions demonstrated to all those around him that he valued, respected and loved women as an honored part of God's creation and His kingdom.

✳ ROADSIDE REFLECTIONS:

• Do you feel any differently about Jesus or about how He might have viewed women after this reading? How does knowing about these interactions between Jesus and women of his time impact your feelings related to your interactions with Him today?

THE NEW TESTAMENT POSITION ON THE STATUS OF WOMEN

Scripture clearly illustrates that this newly founded faith based in the teachings and person of Christ, (now called Christianity) operated under the principles of inclusion and egalitarianism. Both principles were taught and followed while Jesus walked this earth as well as within the foundational years of the early church (Luke 6:20- 30, John 13:14-15, Acts 4:32, Philippians 2:6, James 2:1-5). One remarkable change that provided inclusion of non-Jews and females was the shift from the long practiced Jewish religious ritual of circumcision as the primary religious rite for acceptance and inclusion to the use of believer's baptism (Matthew 3:13-17, Matthew 28:18-20, Mark 16:15). According to Paul's instructions, Gentile Followers of the gospel teachings could circumcise themselves spiritually by their repentance from sin and obedience to the Holy Spirit (Colossians 2:11-12). Physical circumcision of converts was not necessary. This shift from a religious rite that could be obeyed exclusively by Jewish males (Genesis 17:9-14, Acts 7:8) to the more inclusive practice of baptism meant that those of non-Jewish descent as well as women could now become full members of the community and be given the same rights and standing as the men of Jewish lineage (Galatians 3:28). Women weren't just granted marginal access as members of the early church community. Scripture indicates that many women were active participants who were fully involved in the ministry of the New Testament church. For example, women are listed as being among those praying in the upper room before the day of Pentecost (Acts 1:14). They were also among those to speak with unknown tongues after the promised coming of the Holy Spirit (Acts 2:4-18). Peter explained that this sign was in keeping with an Old Testament prophecy contained in Joel chapter 2 in which the prophet proclaimed that God would pour out His spirit on handmaidens and that their daughters would prophesy (Acts 2:17-18). Women worked alongside men who were often their brothers or their husbands to spread the gospel of Jesus. Some of these women held titles of distinction and occupied recognized positions. Many more did not.

One avenue through which it was possible for a woman to gain position and to support the early church ministry was through the offering of her privately owned home as a place for believers to gather. Gathering places were needed for this new community of believers as formalized structures such as those we meet in today did not come into being until much later in our church history. As a result, wealthy widowed women often owned homes that they opened up to the church body and traveling Apostles during the foundational years of the Gospel. Recall, that under Jewish tradition and the customs of the time, the authority and responsibility over the household belonged to the matriarch of the Jewish family (Proverbs 31). The endowment of their homes gave women direct access to teaching and instruction as well as to a position of power over such things as the scheduling and coordinating of meeting times and places. The women who were the owners of these homes would have helped in the logistics and itineraries of the Apostles coming to town as well as with the publicity and invitations. They might also have been privy to more private and direct interactions with the Apostles as is illustrated in the story of the two sisters Mary and Martha. Jesus visited in their home and conversed with the women in a more intimate setting there.

One married couple referenced by Paul several times in the scriptures that opened their home for church meetings was Priscilla (Prisca) and Acquilla (Acts 18:2, Romans 16:5, 1 Corinthians 16:19). This couple was important enough to the work of the church to be mentioned seven different times within New Testament writing. Significantly, in five of those seven references Priscilla's name is listed before her husband Acquilla. This woman was an active, contributing part of the early Christian community. In Romans 16:3 Paul refers to both members of this couple by name as "co-workers" in his missionary efforts. It is significant to note that Paul lists Priscilla's name first within his reference.

Others examples of women who gained position and recognized status by owning homes that were offered as church gathering places include Tabitha, or Dorcus, from the town of Joppa, whom Paul refers to as a "disciple", (Acts 9:36-42) and Lydia in the city of Philippi (Acts 16:13-15). This second woman operated a house of prayer headquartered in her home. Chloe is the name of another woman who lived in the town of Corinth and who offered her home as a meeting place for the Body of Christ (1 Corinthians 1:11).

Paul was not the only Apostle dependent upon the hospitality of women during his ministry. It was in the home of Mary, the mother of John Mark, that Peter met with members of the early church immediately after his deliverance from prison (Acts 12:12-17). Scripture states that it was this wealthy widowed woman's servant girl, Rhoda, who answered the gate when Peter arrived (Acts 12:13).

TRAVELING IN THE COMPANY OF A FEW GOOD WOMEN

Romans Chapter 16 contains the benediction or closing remarks for the letter that the Apostle Paul wrote to the church residing in Rome. This particular passage is distinctive among Paul's writing because of its lengthiness and because it is within this passage that Paul greets many female believers by name. The fact that Paul individually records the names of specific women and praises them publicly within this closing passage should be noted as he has often been accused of displaying misogynist attitudes within his other writing regarding women and church order or structure. Within this text he respectfully calls these women whom he honors his "co-workers" and "fellow prisoners". Paul praises these women for their diligence and hard work on behalf of the spread of the gospel and the work of the church. He greets Priscilla, Junia, and Julia by name and makes reference of Nereus' sister (Romans 16:3, 7, 15). Each of the women named in this particular group traveled in pairs along with their brothers of husbands as missionaries. Paul salutes Tryphena and Tryphosa, whom any Biblical scholars believe were sisters, and refers to these women as laboring for the Lord's work (Romans 16:12) (Maclaren, A., 2003). Persis is also thanked for her labor within the same verse as the sisters and Mary is thanked by Paul for her labor earlier in his discourse in Romans 16:6. In verse 13, Paul regards Rufus's mother affectionately as if she were his own.

Two women of particular interest to Biblical scholars that Paul mentions in this benediction are Phebe (Romans 16:1-2) and Junia (Romans 16:7). These women are distinguished by Paul because he ascribes titles of position to each that many church leaders and historians have felt were to be exclusively reserved for men. Phebe is called a "deacon" to the church at Cenchrea and is commended by Paul as he urges the believers at Rome to support her in any way that she requests.

Junia's name is mentioned only once in the entire New Testament and yet in doing so Paul distinguishes her as an "apostle of note" for her missionary work. Due to this distinction, some early argument existed among scholars over the actual sex of Junia. Some translated the name "Junias" or "Junius" which were both common names given to males of Roman descent (Brooten, B. 1977, p.141-142). However it would seem strange that only one man's name would be listed among all these women of note in Paul's benediction. No scholarly evidence has been given to substantiate the claim that Junia was in fact a man. There is agreement among scholars today that Junia is indeed the only female within the gospels to be given the distinction of "Apostle" (Brooten, B. 1977, p.142).

Such admiration and respect for the labor of women on behalf of the Gospel cannot be the writing of someone who hated, disrespected or sought to oppress women. Paul valued the work of women on behalf of the gospel because he saw the results of that labor first-hand even before his conversion. Several passages recounting Saul's persecution of believers prior to his conversion on the road to Damascus (Acts 9:3-22) state that he had both men and women imprisoned for their faith. Paul also sought out both men and women for slaughter (Acts 8:3, 9:2). Paul confessed to these actions himself when he presented his defense address after being arrested (Acts 22:4). Paul would not have persecuted women if he had not seen them as a threat or as a powerful tool for expanding this new religious movement. Yet , we see that Saul, the zealot, treated women equally under the law; while Paul, the apostle, recognized the value of their labor for the Lord.

SOME SCRIPTURES TO HELP WITH STATUS CONFIRMATION:

"You are all sons of God through faith in Christ Jesus, for all of you who were baptized into Christ have clothed yourselves with Christ. There is neither Jew nor Greek, slave nor free, male nor female, for you are all one in Christ Jesus. If you belong to Christ, then you are Abraham's seed, and heirs according to the promise."- Galatians 3:26-29

The set of verses found in Galatians chapter 3 and printed above strongly abolish any idea that racial, class, or sexual discrimination can be acceptable within the body of Christ. As readers of this text today, we don't know that Paul was particularly interested in gaining equal status for females when he wrote these verses, but that is precisely what his writing accomplishes. In these verses, Paul suggests that there can be no difference in the treatment of the members of God's kingdom based upon race, national origin, class status or biological sex.

While it is true that the primary focus of Paul's missionary ministry was in delivering the good news of the gospel to the non-Jewish world and that Paul's writing throughout the book of Galatians dealt primarily with the question of whether or not Gentiles must go through the rite of circumcision in obedience to Jewish Law before they could become Christians; he did not stop in this dissertation in Galatians with the inclusion of Greeks alone. The fact that Paul includes not only Greeks but also slaves and females in these verses affirms that through faith in Jesus Christ the members of these additional social groups are guaranteed equal access and status along with their Jewish male counterparts. A close examination of Paul's writing, including these verses in Galatians, offers us insight into his personal attitude of egalitarianism towards all people-including women. Paul offered stern warnings to human masters and people of authority who did not treat those under their authority with respect or proper care. He warns masters who are members of God's kingdom to remember their master in heaven when treating those placed under their care (Ephesians 6:9). He also warns that God shows no favoritism in his judgment of those who do wrong (Colossians 3:25).

Paul also had specific instruction and strong words for Christian men regarding how they should treat their wives. In Ephesians 5:25-27 He told men that they are to: "*love your wives, just as Christ loved the church and gave himself up for her to make her holy, cleansing her by the washing with water through the word, and to present her to himself as a radiant church, without stain or wrinkle or any other blemish, but holy and blameless.*" Such love would never condone the beatings, stoning and other unspeakable treatment of women being encouraged from some religious pulpits and lecterns of today. Such teaching could not have been presented from someone following the misogynistic ideologies of which Paul has been falsely accused.

The Cross of Christ Jesus has been called "the great equalizer" because under its shadow we are all equally guilty and all equally forgiven. Paul argues that keeping the law does not bring us into the body of believers. Being a Christian, according to Paul's teaching, was no longer about keeping law (circumcision) but about accepting Christ's sacrifice in faith. It is through the cross of Jesus that we all have equal access to God's throne. Salvation is not the result of being a law abiding Jew but is the free gift of Jesus made available to everyone who expresses faith in Him. The Apostle Peter likewise recognized this fact and expressed this teaching when he assured his listeners that: *"I now realize how true it is that God does not show favoritism but accepts men from every nation who fear him and do what is right."*(Acts 10:34-35). According to Peter's teaching, God is no respecter of persons in offering His gift of salvation or His acceptance into His kingdom.

The following are some additional scriptures that are offered as helpful resources for carefully considering the value and esteem of women within the early Christian church and what should be their value and esteem within the body of Christ today.

1 Peter 1:17-23

"Since you call on a Father who judges each man's work impartially, live your lives as strangers here in reverent fear. For you know that it was not with perishable things such as silver or gold that you were redeemed from the empty way of life handed down to you from your forefathers, but with the precious blood of Christ, a lamb without blemish or defect. He was chosen before the creation of the world, but was revealed in these last times for your sake. Through him you believe in God, who raised him from the dead and glorified him, and so your faith and hope are in God. Now that you have purified yourselves by obeying the truth so that you have sincere love for your brothers, love one another deeply, from the heart. For you have been born again, not of perishable seed, but of imperishable, through the living and enduring word of God."

James 1:5-7:

"If any of you lacks wisdom, he should ask God, who gives generously to all without finding fault, and it will be given to him. But when he asks, he must believe and not doubt, because he who doubts is like a wave of the sea, blown and tossed by the wind. That man should not think he will receive anything from the Lord."

Joel 2:28-29:

"And afterward, I will pour out my Spirit on all people. Your sons and daughters will prophesy, your old men will dream dreams, your young men will see visions. Even on my servants, both men and women, I will pour out my Spirit in those days."

1 Corinthians 2:12-14:

"We have not received the spirit of the world but the Spirit who is from God, that we may understand what God has freely given us. This is what we speak, not in words taught us by human wisdom but in words taught by the Spirit, expressing spiritual truths in spiritual words. The man without the Spirit does not accept the things that come from the Spirit of God, for they are foolishness to him, and he cannot understand them, because they are spiritually discerned."

Hebrews 4:16:

"Let us then approach the throne of grace with confidence, so that we may receive mercy and find grace to help us in our time of need."

Genesis 1:27-28:

"So God created man in his own image, in the image of God he created him; male and female he created them. God blessed them and said to them, "Be fruitful and increase in number; fill the earth and subdue it. Rule over the fish of the sea and the birds of the air and over every living creature that moves on the ground."

✷ ROADSIDE REFLECTIONS:

- Are there other scriptures that you would add to the list of those to confirm your first-class reservation and status?

- How does knowing about these powerful women of ministry that Paul praises within his benediction change your opinion about "women's ministry" within the body?

♛

CHAPTER 5

Packing the Garment Bag

Now that we have established our travel status, confirmed our reservation and gotten our seat assignment we can finally start packing our necessary garments, documents and accessories. The first piece of luggage we will examine in preparation for our upcoming journey is our garment bag. This is the bag that will hold all of our formal or dress clothing, business attire and other important or official apparel.

Our new position as ambassadors for God's heavenly kingdom will certainly demand a new look. The good news is that all that we need to be rightly representative of the kingdom of God has been freely given to us as part of our inheritance. Just for starters, as we gaze at the trousseau spread before us we see that Our Father has given us a **crown of beauty** instead of ashes, **the oil of gladness** instead of mourning, and the **garment of praise** instead of a spirit of despair. He clothes us with **garments of salvation** and arrays us in **a robe of righteousness**. He **adorns our heads** like a priest and as a bride with **jewels** (Isaiah 61:3 a, Isaiah 61:10).

There are certain months of the year that are referred to the sets of 'transitional sales' months within the fashion industry. Magazine editions for these time periods are marked by fashion pages forecasting fur vests and leggings during the dog days of sweltering summer temperatures or editions brimming with full page ads of bronzed bikini clad models as the snow continues piling up on the city streets. In addition to telling savvy shoppers what to buy to get a jump on the trends; these between seasons magazines focus on offering *what to wear now* while waiting for the season to change.

As we gaze down upon those beautiful new clothes that are now part and parcel of our new position, some of us may be feeling as if we are in-between spiritual seasons, or in spiritual transition, at this point in life's journey. We are all new creations but we're living in the same old world. We have a new heavenly home but we're still visiting the old earthly one. We are spiritual beings living and making transactions in a physical world. If, for the *fearfully wonderful woman of God*, life on earth is a business trip representing the heavenly kingdom... then *what in the world do we wear now?* And while it is true that our new position does demand new attire; it is also true, as we all well know, that every new look demands a new attitude. You can't pull it off is you aren't confident wearing it! Being comfortable in a new style of clothing is all about attitude. A girl just acts differently when she paints her nails, curls her hair and puts on a new dress. I suppose that is why it is called "dressing **up**". The manner in which a woman carries herself and the attitude that she exhibits express how she feels about herself on the inside. As ambassadors of Christ and members of God's family, our attitude and the manner in which we carry ourselves should reflect our royal heritage. We are new creations, children of God and joint heirs of His kingdom (2 Corinthians 5:17, Romans 8:17).

When someone becomes a Christian, she becomes a new creation and begins the process of putting off the old nature and of putting on the image of Christ (2 Corinthians 5:17). As an heir of God she has a new family name and a new assignment in the kingdom of God. She is an Ambassador of Christ and a member of a royal priesthood. As such, her new assignment comes with a wardrobe complete with shoes, a crown, jewelry, new robes, and a full set of armor (even the best dressed Barbie doll would be jealous) . After all, it would not do for a daughter of the king to continue on her way dressed in her same old filthy rags or in the clothing that was hurriedly fashioned to cover the shame which she no longer owns (Isaiah 64:4-9, Genesis 3:21).

However, the total transformation of becoming an heir of God and of being completely comfortable in these new clothes will not occur over night. It is a step by step process. We inherit our royal garments at the moment of adoption into the family of God but then we grow into them. We must learn how to put on our robes, claim our inheritance, and walk in them much like we learn how to move with elegance and grace in a pair of high heels. The good news is that it is God who does the transforming and the process of change is initiated by the Holy Spirit as we surrender our life to His control and learn to be sensitive to His leading. The wording used in 2 Corinthians 3:17-18, to describe this process is that of "*beholding as in a mirror the glory of the Lord*" and then "*being transformed into the same image from glory to glory*". Now, before we assume that according to this scripture a new ambassador can just sit back and let the transformation occur rather like sitting in the hairdresser's chair waiting for the cosmetologist to do her magic let's be assured that it doesn't work that way. It's not a magic mirror and it always truthful. And the Holy Spirit is not our fairy godmother. While it is true that Jesus' face is always in that mirror and that God always sees his son's reflection when He looks at me; it is also true that my actions and behaviors can cloud that reflection so that others who are walking on this earth with me don't always see Christ's glory as sharply or as clearly as they could (*James 1:22-25*). We are co-laborers together with God in this process and as such we must choose to be sensitive to the Holy Spirit and choose to be willing to make the necessary adjustments. The Lord will not force us to do anything. It is the Holy Spirit who makes the necessary changes in us, but only when we are willing to open ourselves up to God and to be obedient to His instructions.

Our part of the transformation process of becoming more like Christ and of growing into our inherited position is that of changing our attitude from a rebellious and sinful one to a willing and responsive one. We could just try on all these fabulous new clothes much like a little girl playing dress up or we can recognize that actually "pulling off" these new clothes will require a new attitude. If we decide upon the second choice then before we pack up our newly inherited clothing into our garment bags we will first need to rid ourselves of our old nature and make the necessary adjustments so that our spiritual clothing will fit rather than feel awkward. Scripture tells us to "*put off the old self*" and to be "*made new in the attitude of your minds*" (Ephesians 4:22). This part of the transformation is our job. We must be willing to take off the old person and to strip down totally naked before The Holy Spirit. It is then that we learn how to walk in our new position, our new family name and our God-given authority. Before we can pack our newly inherited clothes into our garment bag and begin the process of becoming fearfully female and wonderfully woman we will need to first remove those attitudes that we have previously stuffed into our bags when we were operating as our old self. It is only in ridding ourselves of our old nature and making the necessary attitude adjustments that we will become more of a reflection of Jesus Christ. If we're going to pull off our new heavenly clothing we are going to need the right attitude.

ADOPTING AN AMBASSADOR'S ATTITUDE

Ever notice that a negative attitude can be a highly contagious thing? One bad attitude or sour disposition can infect a group of eighth grade girls faster than an outbreak of the stomach flu. Likewise, a solitary person with a negative vibe can suck the life right out of an entire group and squelch any feelings of joy gasping for air and trying to hang on to life.

Like it or not, our attitude is a matter of choice and a large part of our attitude is determined based upon where we choose to focus our thoughts and our energy. Attitude is the product of our interpretation of life events and our subsequent response to that interpretation. A new attitude demands a shift in focus and the adoption of a perspective. This is why Ephesians 4:22 tells us that the new woman must change her "attitude of mind". We may not be able to change our circumstances but we can choose how we will respond to them.

If there's one thing that is certain as we begin our travel toward transformation it is that change **is** coming. While many of these changes that take place will be welcomed and exciting; some will not be as we had hoped or envisioned. Some will not arrive on our preferred time schedule. Some changes will not be what WE had in mind AT ALL. Other changes will be downright difficult or devastating. As with any journey, we can choose to enjoy our trip through life or we can choose to be miserable and as a result make all those around us miserable as well.

If we examine our options we see that we are left with very few reasonable choices. We cannot ignore the obvious; which is that the scenery changes on a trip; and, for the better or the worse, so does the traveler. That is why the correct attitude for an ambassador of God will require a certain amount of flexibility and openness... towards others, toward herself and toward her God.

Obstinacy won't get us anywhere. We all know that we will not progress by refusing to budge or by demanding to remain in the same place. No traveler ever got anywhere by digging in her heels and refusing to take another step. Refusing to budge or to make changes will not be an effective way to approach our life or our spiritual transformation.

Impatience will not make the journey any easier or hurry anything along either. Many of us can remember being eleven or twelve and counting down the days until wearing our first bra. Never mind whether a bra was actually needed, we just WANTED one. We might recall, when around that same age, feeling as if we were the only girl in school not allowed to shave her legs. How many of us experienced the sting and discomfort of razor burn or of a nicked back of the ankle after sneaking into the bathroom without permission and hacking up our legs? If only we could learn sooner rather than later that our impatience comes with a price.

✳ ROADSIDE REFLECTIONS:

- People initiate and we respond. Children initiate and we respond. As women, we respond to touch, to words, to sounds, to subtle physical cues, to unspoken communication that men often don't even pick up on... and sometimes our response is not the greatest response possible. These undesirable responses that are derived from SELF (more on that later) result in sin. The little babies listed below in particular are our most common "travel pests". They can burrow in and tag along like bed bugs, fleas and ticks. They are parasites and they feed on and totally devour our joy and contentment.

I would like to suggest that we examine our travel baggage to see if any of these little critters are being harbored in our knapsacks and then see if we can find a way to let go of them before we head out. This will allow for more room for the new responses God is going to provide us. Listed below are the seven little critters that I most often find traveling with me. Are there others that you would add to the list?

- 1)resentment
- 2) anxiety/ distrust
- 3) fear of abandonment
- 4) fear of rejection
- 5) bitterness
- 6) jealousy/coveting
- 7) manipulative spirit

MAKING A TOTAL TRANSFORMATION

As God's designer creation we are made in His image. We are tripartite beings just as he is a tripartite being. That is to say, we are composed of three distinct yet connected parts: body, soul and spirit. Many of us understand the body (physical container/tent) and the spirit (the God part or the eternal being) but we aren't really sure how to make the distinction between the spirit and the soul. It is particularly important as women that we do understand our "soulish" being since females have a very strong connection to this part of our being and tend to respond with it first and to operate in this aspect of our being most often. Popular culture speaks of *women's intuition* or a *woman's way of knowing*. We also speak of women being *in touch* with others and having a higher level of empathy, nurturing and compassion than men. Each of these phrases says something about the soulish part of women.

Our soul is the component of our being that contains our feelings, our responses or our will and what is often commonly referred to as our personality. It is this facet of our being that must be controlled, submitted and transformed before any true ambassador's attitude can appear or be reflected in our mirror (Galatians 2:20). Our emotions must be disciplined and submitted to the Spirit of God if we are going to operate in the mind of Christ and interpret our daily life from God's perspective. Yielding to the Lord and submitting to His Spirit does not mean that we must deny or bury what we are feeling or that we become an emotionless robot or automaton. Christ responded to life situations with faith and with a scriptural perspective. He never reacted out of his emotions or based upon his feelings. Yes, he owned and openly displayed emotions but he never allowed those emotions to dictate his response or to determine his perspective. Likewise, if we are going to be ambassadors of God's kingdom and going to reflect the same attitude that was in Christ Jesus; then we must choose to face the facts of life with faith and truth and ask God to take care of our feelings. Our emotions are not to be ignored; only to be secondary and submitted.

We must also be careful not to confuse emotions for discernment. God's ambassadors are told that we must worship Him in Spirit and in truth (John 4:24). Scripture never instructs us to worship God with our emotional response or from the center or our emotional being. Feelings are an important part of our physical being. They greatly affect our psychological and physical well-being (for the good and the bad). They operate right alongside our physical and spiritual being; but the three parts of our being do not always operate in unity or agreement. Often our emotions will deceive us and contradict the truth of God's word. Relying upon our emotions to guide us can lead us to doubt and into sin. Our emotions can only be in agreement with God's purpose and plan when they are surrendered to His Spirit's control. Having a "hunch" or a "gut feeling" is not the same as being led by God and true spiritual insight or discernment will never contradict an instruction contained within God's word. We must not rely upon our emotional response as an indication of God's purpose or His will.

As followers of Jesus Christ, we are instructed that our attitude should be the same as the one He exhibited while living here on earth and interacting with human beings as well as with His Heavenly Father (Philippians 2:5). If we are going to wear the attitude of Christ, then there will be no room in our garment bag for the soulish emotions of insensitivity, hardness, bitterness, malice, resentment, indifference or a host of other favorite reactions we may be presently carrying with us (Ephesians 4:31-32). Those are all attitudes reflected by our former self and as such are easily swayed or tempted by the desires of the flesh and/or the difficulty of the situation. They respond in an effort to protect the person, their investments, rights or interests. God does not desire for us to follow Him based upon our feelings or soulish being. He requires that we submit to Him based upon faith and the fact of His word. The wonderfully woman's suitcase contains the new attitude that is exhibited through gentleness, goodness, meekness, patience and self-control (Galatians 5:22-23). These are all fruits of the Spirit not reactions of the flesh.

The truth is, nobody will know what our attitude is until we put it on display or exhibit it openly. That happens when we come in contact with those people or things that irritate, frustrate or otherwise stretch us beyond our own capacity to tolerate, ignore or endure. Remember, an attitude is the outward manifestation of our true inward being. We are wearing our insides on display on our outside through the attitude that we exhibit. While it may be possible to put on a false attitude, to fake a smile, or to pretend a demeanor to deceive those around us, it is impossible to deceive God. He knows our real response and attitude because He knows our inward being and searches our hearts (Psalm 44:21, I Samuel 16:7, Proverbs 23:7). A true attitude adjustment will occur only when we begin to apply the discipline of scripture to our thought life and our emotions and then willingly put on the mind of Christ. We must choose to begin to filter our fleshly attitude through Christ's teachings and model our behaviors using his. Having the mind of Christ will allow us to have his response (attitude) to the people, places and events of our lives. It will also let us think in complete unity with the Holy Spirit and then be transformed into his image. As His ambassadors we *can* have His attitude because we have His mind available to us. With the mind of Christ we *can* take every negative attitude or thought that trips us up, hold it captive and then demolish every argument that is contrary to God's truth or that doesn't agree with his mind (perspective) (2 Corinthians 10:5&6).

Putting on a Christ- like attitude will require that we discipline our feelings and emotions and determine to interpret things from God's perspective. The purpose of God's word is not to strengthen our soulish feelings; it is to encourage our faith. Our Father will not strengthen our feelings to enable us to trust him. He requires that we put our emotional responses in proper perspective and that we be willing to trust Him regardless of our feelings.

Being able to wear this newly required Christ-like attitude begins only after having established a personal and connected relationship with God. Being more like Christ requires developing intimacy with Him. We can only learn Christ's attitudes and responses in the same way as His disciples did. That is by being in His presence and spending time with Him. In Matthew 11:29 Jesus invites His disciples to come and learn from Him. He states that He is gentle and humble in heart and He promises that it is with him that we will find rest for our souls. Our personal transformation begins when we accept this invitation. What we learn while spending time with Jesus can never be taken from us (Luke 10:42).

MAKING AN ATTITUDE ADJUSTMENT

How do we, as ambassadors of God's kingdom, shift from displaying our old attitudes to displaying an attitude that reflects the new fearfully wonderful us? The first step in the process is being willing to change. That requires being open to the notion that what we are doing now isn't really working for us. We must be willing to lay our old self aside and recognize that what God desires for us is best. We must determine that we are deserving of God's best and then be willing to accept His gentle correction. The first step in the process is our repentance. Then we move to obedience and inspiration, and finally to modeling in our outer being what God has placed in our inner being. We can all become everything that God intended for us to be as His designer creation (Psalms 139:14-16). We can trust ourselves completely to the one who died for us and to the Creator who has a perfect plan for our lives (John 3:16, Jeremiah 29:10-11).

1. Evaluating Our Present Attitudes

There are a number of things that can influence our attitude, control our minds and emotions, and hold our thoughts captive. These could range from hurtful encounters with others to a television show we watched, a book we read or the lyrics of some song that we just can't seem to get out of our heads. The resulting responses can run the gamut from depression to lust or jealousy, insecurity, frustration, anger or even becoming indifferent or closed off to the hurts and needs of those around us. A true attitude change to that of an ambassador will require that we submit all those former thoughts and emotional responses to the Lord. He cannot do anything in us against our will. God will not force us to change. Each of us must determine to put off our old self willingly (Galatians 2:20). We must be willing to open ourselves up to the Lord's correction and leading as we confess those fleshly responses. We must ask Him to eliminate those old responses and to replace them with His Spirit's fruit (Galatians 5:22-26).We can submit ourselves and become vulnerable to his leading by remembering that He loves us and desires to transform us to His image for our benefit as well as for his glory. We can start the transformation of putting on our new self by meditating on the following scriptures and asking the Holy Spirit to strengthen the desire to change within us.

"Casting down arguments and every high thing that exalts itself against the knowledge of God, bringing every thought into captivity to the obedience of Christ..." 2 Corinthians 10:5. *Remember immediate emotional responses are rarely reliable.*

"Create in me a pure heart, O God, and renew a steadfast spirit within me". Psalm51:10

"Search me, O God, and know my heart; test me and know my anxious thoughts. See if there is any offensive way in me, and lead me in the way everlasting". Psalm 139:23-24

2. Choosing to Change Our Focus

If we choose to dwell on the negative, our attitude will reflect the same. Negativity begets negativity. Remember attitude is a reflection. It mirrors our insides on our outsides. What we focus on is interpreted through our emotions and filtered into our inner being where it is then reflected in our outer person's behaviors, words and reactions. Shifting our focus to the things that glorify God will strengthen our faith and help to align our emotions to reflect His character and to follow His will. Aligning our fleshly responses to reflect God's character will require that we apply the disciplines and teachings of scripture to our thoughts and that we allow those instructions to govern our emotional responses. Doing so will require lining our behavior up with what the scripture teaches us is right even when we don't feel like it. Developing this discipline of the flesh will not be easy as the flesh doesn't like to be denied. Just remember how difficult it is to be on a diet and to try not to eat chocolate cake when it is readily available and smelling so delicious. The moment that we determine to surrender our flesh to the instructions of the Lord we can anticipate that temptation will follow.

- *"Finally, brethren, whatever things are true, whatever things are noble, whatever things are just, whatever things are pure, whatever things are lovely, whatever things are of good report, if there is any virtue and if there is anything praiseworthy; meditate on these things."* -Philippians 4:8

- *"Love is patient, love is kind. It does not envy, it does not boast, it is not proud. It is not rude, it is not self-seeking, it is not easily angered, and it keeps no record of wrongs. Love does not delight in evil but rejoices with the truth. It always protects, always trusts, always hopes, and always perseveres. Love never fails."* -1Corinthians 13:4-8

- *"Love must be sincere. Hate what is evil; cling to what is good. Be devoted to one another in brotherly love. Honor one another above yourselves. Never be lacking in zeal, but keep your spiritual fervor, serving the Lord. Be joyful in hope, patient in affliction, and faithful in prayer. Share with God's people who are in need. Practice hospitality. Bless those who persecute you; bless and do not curse. Rejoice with those who rejoice; mourn with those who mourn. Live in harmony with one another. Do not be proud, but be willing to associate with people of low position. Do not be conceited. Do not repay anyone evil for evil. Be careful to do what is right in the eyes of everybody. If it is possible, as far as it depends on you, live at peace with everyone. Do not take revenge, my friends, but leave room for God's wrath, for it is written: 'It is mine to avenge; I will repay,' says the Lord. On the contrary: 'If your enemy is hungry, feed him; if he is thirsty, give him something to drink. In doing this, you will heap burning coals on his head.' Do not be overcome with evil, but overcome evil with good."* - Romans 12:9-21

3. Putting on The Mind of Christ

The mind of Christ is readily available to each of us as part of our royal inheritance. It is ours to pick up and to include with our other royal robes in our garment bag. However, having the mind of Christ safely tucked into our bag is not enough. Simply packing a bicycle helmet into our athletic bag or hanging it off our handle bars will not protect our heads should we take a tumble. We must choose to fasten it to our noggins for it to have any benefit. Likewise, having the mind of Christ is of no value to us unless we choose to wear it.

Wearing the mind of Christ will mean that anything that infiltrates our mind and seeks to influence our thought life or emotions and the resulting attitude will first be filtered through Christ's way of thinking and responding. The mind of Christ operates much like a heavenly spam and virus filter to protect our brain's internal processor and emotional programming systems. Anyone who is wearing the mind of Christ cannot think in a way that is counter to scripture or react in a "fleshly" manner without setting off an internal alarm or alert sounded by the Holy Spirit. When the alarm sounds we are given the opportunity to capture the infiltrating thought, to surround it with God's truth, and to align it with scripture *before* it produces an undesired, sinful response. Using the mind of Christ during times of frustration enables us to speak His truth over ourselves and to expose the enemy's lies. As a result, our relationship with God is strengthened and His truth helps us to stand in our inherited authority as His daughters. The mind of Christ reminds us that we are God's daughters and as such He desires what is best for our lives (Galatians 4:4-7). As Heirs we can ask anything in faith knowing that Our Father will give us that which we ask of Him if it will reflect His presence within us. Focusing on scriptures like those listed below will help us remember who we are in Christ when our faith is tested.

"Ask and it will be given to you; seek and you will find; knock and the door will be opened to you. For everyone who asks receives; he who seeks finds; and to him who knocks, the door will be opened. Which of you, if his son asks for bread, will give him a stone? 10 Or if he asks for a fish, will give him a snake? If you, then, though you are evil, know how to give good gifts to your children, how much more will your Father in heaven give good gifts to those who ask him?"-Matthew 7:7-11

"Let us then approach the throne of grace with confidence, so that we may receive mercy and find grace to help us in our time of need."-Hebrews 4:6

"We walk by faith and not by sight"- 2 Corinthians 5:7

"But the fruit of the Spirit is love, joy, peace, patience, kindness, goodness, faithfulness, gentleness and self-control." -Galatians 5:22-23

"Your attitude should be the same as that of Christ Jesus: Who, being in very nature God, did not consider equality with God something to be grasped, but made himself nothing, taking the very nature of a servant, being made in human likeness. And being found in appearance as a man, he humbled himself and became obedient to death- even death on a cross."- Philippians 2:5-8

"The Lord thy God in the midst of thee is mighty"- Zephaniah 3:17

The process of unpacking the incorrect emotional responses that are controlled by our old fleshly nature and developing the discipline of putting on the mind of Christ to govern our attitude is a lifelong one. Reflecting the attitude of Christ in our interactions with others will require daily attitude checks and adjustments. The Holy Spirit will continue to bring things to our attention that need fine- tuning if we remain sensitive to his nudging and listen for his guidance. We must then choose to respond to these nudgings and to be obedient to The Lord's correction. Each of us is being changed from glory to glory and progressing from image to image as we grow closer to our eternal home. As fearfully wonderful women we should constantly evaluate our present attitudes to see if we are exhibiting ones that reflect Christ's redemptive work in the mirror of our life. Does our outside match the changes occurring in our insides? Thank God that His mercy is new every morning and that He forgives our incorrect attitudes and gives us grace sufficient to meet every life situation (Lamentations 3:22-23, 2 Corinthians 12:9).

✳ ROADSIDE REFLECTIONS:

- Which components of your old wardrobe do you need to unpack from your garment bag (Ephesians 4: 29-32)?

- Which components of the new wardrobe do you need to ask the Lord to help you exhibit more? (Galatians 5:22-23)?

- Do you have any additional scripture that we can all add to our travel journals to ease in our unpacking of the old self?

ASSEMBLING OUR ATTIRE

Our garment bag as royal ambassadors is full enough without our adding to it with any unpacked attitudes and resistant responses derived from our old nature. Assuring that our royal robes fit properly requires that we destroy our old self-righteous attitudes which are nothing more than filthy rags compared to the beautiful silken tapestries with which God desires to clothe His daughters (Isaiah 64:6). When we agree to allow the Holy Spirit to replace those worn out and useless attitudes with the attitude reflected by Christ Jesus we are adorned with Christ's righteousness and reflect his glory. If we take a peek into the garment bags spread before us we will find our royal robes of righteousness as well as the vitally important mind of Christ Jesus safely tucked within. We will also find such royal accessories as our crown of life as well as other bridal jewelry layered between the articles of clothing collected there. The list below includes *some* of the other garments that are our loving Father has provided us as the Bride of Christ, Joint-heirs of the Royal Kingdom, Daughters of the Heavenly Father, Members of the Royal Priesthood of Believers, and Ambassadors of God's Kingdom:

- Isaiah 61:3: The Crown of Beauty and the Garment of Praise
- Isaiah 61:10 Robe of Righteousness
- Isaiah 61:10: Bridal jewels
- Isaiah 61:10: Garments of Salvation
- Psalm 132:9, 1 Peter 2:9 : Priestly robes of righteousness
- Proverbs 31:22: Custom clothes of tapestry, silk and purple
- Luke 14:7-35: Clothes fit for a Marriage Feast
- Luke 22:13-30: A girdle for your loins and work clothes
- 1 Corinthians 9:25:An Everlasting Crown
- Philippians 4:1 : A Soul Winner's Crown
- 2 Timothy 4:8: A Crown of Righteousness
- James 1:12: A Crown of Life
- 1 Peter 5:4 : A Crown of Glory
- 1 Peter 5:5: Humility
- 2 Peter 3:14: Spotless and Pure garments

- Revelation 3:1-6 , 2 Peter 3:14: Spotless and Pure garments
- Revelation 19:7-8: Bridal clothes of Fine linen, clean and white

The list of designer clothing above reads more favorably than anything Galliano, Dior or even Channel is doing this season. It is luxurious, lavish, elegant, cut in silk, fine linen and brocade, and tailored with an impeccable eye for detail. Our Father has thought of everything. He's even included even work clothes and a girdle. If the same God who dressed the lilies of the field and the birds of the air has also designed our eternal, spiritual attire then we should be filled with anticipation waiting to behold the lavish detail and indescribable beauty of it all. How wonderful to stand before his throne clothed in his beauty and wrapped in his great love forever!

The vast collection of spiritual attire provided in our royal inheritance does not end with a full garment bag. There are many more bags to be filled as we continue packing for our journey and we will take a look at outerwear, cosmetics, and foot fashion later in our packing process. This might be a good place to pause and think about what we will wear underneath our beautiful and regal new clothing. After all, a garment's fit relies heavily upon the underpinnings and the foundations supporting it. While ideas about what it means to be properly attired have changed over time; every finished fashion statement is built from the inside out and starts with the correct foundation underneath. Wearing any new garment requires a new attitude and every new attitude requires the proper support. Maybe it's time to discuss our lingerie bag.

✳ ROADSIDE REFLECTIONS:

- Before we get dressed we need to get naked and if we are going to wear our new clothes then all those old attitudes that reflect our old self will need to be unpacked and left behind. We have learned that our attitude is the outward manifestation of our inward being. In a sense, we wear our insides on our outside through our attitude. It will be impossible to put on a false attitude, to fake a smile or to pretend a demeanor to deceive God if we are naked before him (Psalm 44:21, 1 Samuel 16:7, Proverbs 23:7) How does it make you feel to think about being stripped down naked before the Lord?

CHAPTER 6

Our Lingerie Bag:
The case for good foundations.

An undergarment —also known as shape wear, support wear, lingerie, intimate apparel or a foundation- is a piece of clothing designed primarily to be worn under our street clothes. Their chief function is to somehow enhance or improve the wearer's body shape to achieve a more desirable structure or figure upon which to drape a piece of clothing. Stated another way, these garments take on all that 'Mister Gravity' has to offer in an attempt to pull up what has flattened out or fallen down back into its original position. Foundations can be made from a variety of materials ranging from lace and silk to latex or spandex. They are sorted and labeled according to their shape contorting abilities and their level of control. In recent years, the sales of such garments have increased considerably. This could be because the grayer our population becomes the greater our fondness grows for anything that promises to lift and separate or firm, smooth, mold, and otherwise improve the ever aging birthday suit.

Imagine that it is the ever dreaded bathing suit season. There we stand, half-naked, cloistered away behind the draped opening of the department store dressing room. It's only us but we're totally exposed in a full length mirror under the harshest lighting we've ever encountered in our life. What do we see when we gaze longer than a minute into that full length, 360 degree vision enabled mirror? If we're a teen, do we praise our lean legs, slender hips and perky breasts? If we're a young mother arriving at our mid-thirties, do we marvel at the strength of our thighs in their ability to carry a sleeping two year old or a full load of laundry up two flights of stairs at the end of our long day? If we're rounding that corner of life into the fifties, are we amazed at how our body has served us? It has gracefully endured the rigors of pregnancies, sickness, sleepless nights, and other countless many hardships. Are we still feeling "fearfully wonderful" or do our true inner emotions run closer to " fading fast " or "fiercely wrinkled"? What are the foundations carefully packed away in your lingerie bags that are utilized to shape your self-image?

Sadly, if we're like the average American woman these dressing room scenarios are not very likely. General research distributed through The National Institutes of Health concludes that over 90% of women report being dissatisfied with their appearance in some aspect or another. In that dressing room, our focus was more likely on the cellulite and dimples on our thighs than on their strength. As a young girl, we probably wished that we had more "junk in our trunk" or slightly larger breasts to fill out that string bikini in our hands and if we've reached middle aged we probably want to recycle some of that junk and our current bra cup runneth over with excess. Despite what advertisements may be saying about fifty being the new thirty, any honest perimenopausal woman will tell you that gravity's pull has had a direct impact on the image that she now sees reflected in that mirror as she folds her wrinkled body like origami into an extra strength tummy control bathing suit that requires the jaws of life to pull it up beyond her hips. Sooner or later, we all go through the pantyhose dance, the shape wear shuffle or some other hokey pokey in the attempt to squeeze our ever increasing, incessantly wrinkling, constantly decaying earthly tents into a perceived younger, bouncier, tighter, therefore more desirable configuration.

BODY IMAGE, BODY SHAPE AND BODY SIZE

As women, our perceptions of our bodies and the conclusions that we make about whether or not we are attractive form our body image, impact our self-esteem and our influence attitudes. Our idea about how we actually look as compared to how we *ought* to look is influenced by the culture in which we live and interact as well as by the messages, truthful or false, that we choose to believe about ourselves.

Any message that is allowed to permeate our thoughts and to take root will contribute to our "self- talk" or to the messages that we tell ourselves and others about our body and our pleasure or displeasure with it. Healthy and beautiful young women can often hold distorted or poor body images. The self- image she holds will depend upon the messages she receives and the voices to which she listens.

American popular culture places a great deal of emphasis on a woman's appearance and on such issues as her body weight, dress size, and age. Our culture's ideas about beauty and the value of women are often reduced to nothing more than a series of arbitrary numbers. Women have been conditioned to feel good or bad about themselves based upon the number on the scale or on the tag inside the back of their jeans. It has also become socially unacceptable for a woman to boast about her actual age, another number, unless she can trick someone into thinking she is younger or "lie to the camera".

From a very young age females begin to believe that a large portion of their value is derived from their size, their sensuality and their attractiveness. The pressures to be beautiful and thin are intense on young girls within today's society because the media puts the major focus on external characteristics rather than on the inward essence when defining the ideal female. Little girls begin negative self- talk about their bodies very early and many grade school age girls are already dieting.

Images of scantily dressed and provocatively posed female bodies are prolific in advertising as the female form is used to sell anything and everything from tools to toothpaste. Female bodies are dissected into separate and independent parts and media encourages women to focus on a particular aspect of their physical form with distain or displeasure and then to seek to pump it up, slim it down, fill it out or cut it off. And if that weren't enough, the stakes just keep getting higher and higher as the media's portrayal of what is attractive for the ideal female body type keeps getting thinner and thinner. The size difference gap between what is being shown on the run ways and catwalks and what is reality for most women in America grows deeper and wider with each passing fashion year. The average fashion model shown on the pages of the industry's leading magazines is a size 2 while the average American woman is more realistically closer to a size 14. No real female can compete with the photo shopped, air brushed images of these younger and younger cover models who eat only lean protein, work out 4 to 6 hours a day and have had unknown "nips and tucks" along the way. The reality is that even the model in question doesn't look the way she does on that cover without a great deal of help. Statistically, her looks will not last and neither will her health if she continues to live the life style she is now living. Cycles of unhealthy fad dieting, partying and losing necessary sleep due to staying out too late, followed by the consumption of large quantities of caffeine and nicotine will eventually take a toll on a young girl's appearance. It's ironic the unhealthy things that we will do and risks that we will take in an effort to appear more attractive.

Women's magazines are overflowing with articles promising sublime happiness **IF** we can just lose those last ten pounds, tighten our rear ends or increase our cup size. The promised reward media offers for discovering *Victoria's secret* is the perfect life: "the happily ever after" we read about in fairy tales, complete with the perfect man, perfect career, perfect home, and two perfect children. Sadly, we buy into the illusion and swallow the lie hook, line and sinker. Women are literally killing themselves through starvation, yo-yo dieting, laxative and diet pill abuse, over exercising, or some other desperate means to achieve this unobtainable goal and to fit into these unrealistic, culturally imposed standards of beauty. The National Association of Anorexia and Associated Disorders estimate that one out of every four college-aged women is using some unhealthy means to lose weight and eating disorders have the highest mortality rate of any mental illness. With statistics that high for college girls alone, it should not be surprising that according to the National Institute of Mental Health the mortality rate associated with anorexia nervosa is 12 times higher than the death rate for all other causes of death for females between the ages of 15 and 24.

SELF-TALK, SATAN AND SCRIPTURE

Based on the current research, it would appear that the end result of choosing to accept the popular culture's message that a woman's self-worth is found in the shape of her body or contained within her sex appeal is not the media's promised "happily ever after" but is that of death, despair and destruction.

For the Christian woman it should be easy to see that such an outcome is not what our Lord promised for our lives. John 10:10 reminds us that: "The thief comes only to steal and kill and destroy". Christ said that he came: "that they may have life, and have it to the full." Based upon this scripture reference alone, we can conclude that any time we see such obvious destruction of the female being and such a high evidence of death related to the performance of a social norm that social norm is not one we need to wholeheartedly embrace. We can also be assured that our enemy, Satan, is at work in it. John 8:44 refers to him as the "Father of all lies". It wouldn't take much to agree that he helped in the spinning and development of this whopper. The question for Christian women becomes just exactly how much stock should we be putting into the world's **value** system (yes, I mean the system that is used to evaluate and value us as women) and how much we are actually being influenced by the voices that we hear and the images that we see.

✳ ROADSIDE REFLECTIONS:

- How do you respond to the notion that your value as a woman has been reduced to a series of arbitrary numbers by our culture? IF honest, how influenced have you been by our society's system of evaluation?

PRETTY LITTLE LIES

Since being cast out of heaven, Satan's number one objective has been to trip up, to hold captive and to defeat the members of the kingdom of God. He does this through any and every means available. His primary tactics are lies and manipulation of the truth. He is a liar and has been a liar since his initial interaction with the first woman, Eve. His purpose in lying to her as well as to us is to destroy the sacred relationship that exists between mankind and Creator God. He desires to pervert God's truth, to isolate us from our loving Father and to leave us hopeless, helpless and destitute in our sin (Genesis 3:4-5, 2 Corinthians 11:3). The ultimate goal of all Satan's lies has been and ever will be the total destruction of God's most beloved creation- human beings. We must not allow our self-talk to be influenced by Satan's lies. Scripture clearly details what happened when the first woman listened to what he had to say... and the outcome wasn't pretty.

The world system through the voices of media such as fashion magazines, Hollywood gossip shows and music lyrics would have women believe that we are flawed and imperfect and that our bodies must be contorted, starved and even surgically altered if they are going to be culturally acceptable works of beauty. Christian women are caught up in a series of lies regarding the importance of the numbers attached to their age, weight, dress size and other components of their physical appearance. We've forgotten that the bathroom scale measures weight and not our intrinsic value. Our dress size does not reflect how we measure in the eyes of the Lord. The world tells us that the greatest part of our value as a female is found in our physical attractiveness and sensuality and does little to discuss the value of the inner being or the beauty of a godly soul. The lie that suggests that women find their value in being sexually desirable and pleasing to men is not only based on an arbitrary and constantly changing standard but is also in direct opposition to the teachings of scripture which tell us that we have been purposefully designed to please our creator and to do His divine will.

"For we are His workmanship, created in Christ Jesus for good works, which God has prepared beforehand that we should walk in them". Ephesians 2:10.

If it is true that the female being was created with intent by God and perfectly equipped by her creator to perform His will and to accomplish His purpose; then isn't it also true that women will find their greatest value in pleasing Him rather than in pleasing our society or males? Recent statistics collected by the Physicians Resource Council indicate that over twenty percent (20%) of adolescent girls have had at least one sexual encounter before their fifteenth birthday. Researchers connect this desire for early sexual experiences directly to such things as the belief that having sex will keep their boyfriend interested in them and that a sexual relationship will provide them with the love they so desperately crave. Other influences included believing that a poor self-image or low self-esteem could be corrected through the increased social popularity that would be achieved through sexual activity. Influences such as television, music and the internet lead teens to conclude that everyone is having sex and that sexual activity is the means to achieve social acceptance (Summerville, Geri (2006). These lies are stealing our daughters of their innocence and contributing to the increase of sexually transmitted diseases, date rape, teenage pregnancy, teen abortion and deep emotional scarring.

Interestingly enough, in the scripture reference used earlier that is found in John 15 Christ states that the world *hates us just as it hated Him*. What then could be the ultimate goal of these worldly voices leading women to self-loathing, poor body image, compulsive dieting and deprivation, eating disorders and a host of other destructive end results? John 10:10 reminds us that: "The thief comes only to steal and kill and destroy". Where ever we see stealing, killing and destruction we know that our enemy is at work.

Christ came to offer life to its fullest. He calls us to be fully female and wonderfully woman and to embrace all that our creator placed within us (Psalm 139:14). This is only possible as we become fully surrendered to Him and to His designed purpose for us. When we apply scriptural principles and truths to understanding what it is to be female we learn that to be fearfully and wonderfully female is to be glorious and unique in every detail. Fabulous females come in all sorts of heights, shapes, sizes and colors. Each of us is as unique as the lilies of the field and the birds in the sky (Matthew 6: 26-29). Being uniquely his and uniquely us offers an opportunity to display the artistic majesty of our Creator. Each of us is His designer creation. We were formed by Him and are being transformed by Him. Our life, our journey, our very existence are all held in His hand. We have only but to get in touch with Him and to communicate with Him to change our destructive self - talk to words of hope, promise and life. It is only through intimately knowing Him that we can establish a true concept of who we are. The more intimately we know Him and what his word says about us, the more secure and firm is our foundation.

As followers of Christ we are commanded to speak the truth in love (Ephesians 4:15) and are told not to lie because doing so is an act of our old sinful nature or attitude (Colossians 3:9+10). This scriptural principle would apply not only to the words that we speak to others, but to the lies that we tell ourselves. Too often we accept the lies and half-truths of our culture as truth and choose to carry their weight with us on our life journey. What we choose to believe about who we are and about how we are created is foundational to how we will carry out our new position as ambassadors of God's kingdom. Our robes of righteousness will fit best with the proper foundation of truth. We must be evaluated based on more than an arbitrary series of numbers. Our value to God as His respected and cherished creation is far greater than that.

ROADSIDE REFLECTIONS:

- What scriptures or truths do you have readily available for reassurance of your true beauty on those fat days, bad hair days and blah feeling days?
- In this reading I brought up the issue of our enemy and his part in our destructive self- talk. Satan is called the *accuser*

of the brethren and the *Father of Lies* and as such He will try to bring up false accusations and untruths against believers to other as well as to the believer herself (1 Peter 2:12, 3:16, Revelations 12:10). Hurtful words such as "You're ugly", "Nobody loves you", and "You don't measure up" can originate from the mouths of others whom we admire and respect (our parents, other children, role models) and from influences within our culture (media, music, television). These hurtful words and evaluations that originated outside of us can very quickly become our own thoughts and self-talk to ourselves and about ourselves. While it is a serious matter when the enemy or another person brings false accusations against God's beloved it is a particularly serious matter when we bring those accusations and hurtful statements against ourselves internally. Such destructive self-talk will lead to unhealthy attitudes, behaviors and self-image. It may also lead to jealousy, resentment and bitterness against God. How do we turn down all those outside voices to hear the voice of God as we evaluate ourselves?

"Therefore everyone who hears these words of mine and puts them into practice is like a wise man who built his house on the rock. The rain came down, the streams rose, and the winds blew and beat against that house; yet it did not fall, because it had its foundation on the rock. But everyone who hears these words of mine and does not put them into practice is like a foolish man who built his house on sand. The rain came down, the streams rose, and the winds blew and beat against that house, and it fell with a great crash."- Matthew 7:24-27

Cultural standards and definitions of beauty will change from time period to time period and from place to place. Evaluating oneself by those standards is comparable to trying to build a house on quick sand. God's standards do not change. They are not shifting sand. We can trust His evaluation of us because of our value as His respected and cherished creation. Most importantly, we can see our bodies as objects of great beauty because God chose to make our physical bodies our physical bodies His holy dwelling place.

*"Do you not know that your body is a temple of the Holy
Spirit, who is in you, whom you have received from God?
You are not your own; you were bought at a price. Therefore
honor God with your body". -1 Corinthians 6:19-20*

Certainly the God of the universe would not choose to make his holy habitat in an inferior, defiled or otherwise defective dwelling. Note the scripture refers to our bodies as God's temple. Think about the beauty, majesty and splendid architecture of the temples to which the author of that time period would have been referencing. Such refined and elegant structures would be considered anything but second rate. Many have stood the test of time and are still standing today as monuments of praise to the God in whose honor they were erected. Their age has only gilded their gold and refined their beauty and elegance. These structures have become even more valuable and are judged more beautiful with the passing of time. So it is with a godly woman. Age should refine her beauty and add to it not diminish it. The grace, discernment and wisdom that come with age combined with time spent in prayer and godly service can only increase the beauty and the value of a godly woman.

�֎ ROADSIDE REFLECTIONS:

So... if we're being honest... which number carries the most influence over you? Is it the number on the tag in your jeans (size)? The number on the scale (weight)? The number on your driver's license (age)? Some other number? The three things that women lie about the most are: their age, their weight and the number of sex partners they have had. They even lie to themselves about such things as the number of calories that they consumed in a day or their level of debt, still more numbers. How do you relate to this numbers game? Are you always honest about weight, size, etc.?

Hopefully, we can now see why it is so vital for women to have the right attitude about their bodies as the foundation to their self-image and sense of worth. Knowing that God created our bodies with purpose, reverence and respect helps us to understand how valuable we are to Him. Zephaniah 3:17 states that God takes great delight in us, that He quiets us with His Love and that He joys over us with singing. How wonderful to imagine God humming to himself while working over His creation called woman!

BASIC FOUNDATIONS TO SUPPORT YOUR AMBASSADOR'S ROBES

Listed below are some simple, liberating, and yet affirming foundations that each of us will want to include in our lingerie bags as the underpinning and support for the inherited garments that we packed in our garment bags.

1. God created each of us with a divine purpose and a plan for our lives. We are His designer creation. He alone knows that perfect niche He desires us to fill. His plan for us includes working in and through our physical bodies. We are each His temple (Genesis 50:20, Jeremiah 29:10-11, John 10:10; Romans 8:28, Romans 12:1-2). We need to determine to be a glorious structure designed for his praise and glory.

2. We have already established that Satan is aware of our potential and that he seeks to destroy our lives as well as our relationship with God. Jesus personally reminded Peter that Satan was desiring to destroy us all but that Christ himself prays for us. As fearfully wonderful women of God, we need to flee anything that sounds like one of the enemy's lies or that fulfills an ungodly appetite found within our old nature. We must remember to filter our responses through the mind of Christ (Proverbs 14:12, Luke 22:31-34 Galatians 5:16- 21, 1 John 4:1-6).

3. Our key scripture found in Psalms 139:1-16 tells us that God designed our physical features and characteristics in accordance to His plan for each of us before we were born. He gave each of us unique talents, gifts and capabilities so that we might be His work of art and glorify Him in all we do. (Psalm 119:73, Psalm 139, Job 10:8-9, Isaiah 45:9, Isaiah 62:2-3). We need to focus on the beauty of His creation rather than the flaws or imperfections that we might see in comparing ourselves to our culture's standards for physical beauty.

4. We are each a work in progress. We are a potentiality and we have a hope and a future! We are being transformed from glory to glory as we submit to His design plans and to His creative power. We may not see the outcome of his plan but He has one for each of us (Psalm 138:8, Jeremiah 29:10-11, Zephaniah 9:16, Ephesians 2:10; 4:24, 2 Corinthians 5:17).

We need to be gracious to ourselves and to have patience with our seemingly slow progress.

5. Our creator determines our beauty by searching and transforming our inward being. We reflect the beauty He gives us by seeking to display the attributes that our creator has placed within us as well as to reflect the character of Jesus. (1Samuel 16:7, Matthew 15:11, 1 Corinthians 6:17-20, Galatians 5:22-23). God knows our hearts and true person. He designed our inward being (Psalm 139:13). We have his treasure in these clay vessels (2 Corinthians 4:7).

6. Our greatest fulfillment in life comes by being His unique creation and being set apart for His service. (1 Pet. 2:9, Romans 15:9, 1 Corinthians 6: 13-20). We are truly free to be unique and different and need to conform only to His desired image rather than the one presented in a magazine, movie, music video or television show.

7. As ambassadors of God's heavenly kingdom and members of His family, what we wear and our physical appearance does have a direct bearing on Our Lord's reputation. People read us and draw conclusions from what they see. Our appearance sends messages about ourselves and about our Lord. We need to be sensitive to our witness when we dress and interact with others while being aware of the entanglements of legalism. (Acts1:1-8, Matthew 28:18-20, John 7:7, Romans 10:15, Galatians 5:19-21). We can rely upon the Holy Spirit to speak to us if something is inappropriate for us.

Psalm 139: 13-16

[13] For you created my inmost being;
you knit me together in my mother's womb.
[14] I praise you because I am fearfully and wonderfully made;
your works are wonderful,
I know that full well.
[15] My frame was not hidden from you
when I was made in the secret place.
When I was woven together in the depths of the earth,
[16] your eyes saw my unformed body.
All the days ordained for me
were written in your book
before one of them came to be.

CHAPTER 7

The Shoe bag

*"How beautiful are thy feet with shoes, O prince's daughter!
The joints of thy thighs are like jewels, the work of the hands
of a cunning workman."*- Song of Solomon 7:1

Many of us will admit that our love of shoes began with a tiny little pair of plastic heeled, elastic strapped, pink high heels lovingly placed on our feet by our mothers. Some of us clickity- clacked in those dime store treasures from the time that we were three and have loved the sound of heels ever since. From the type she wears to the number of pairs, a girl's shoes tell a great deal about her. They might indicate what she does for a living, how much money she makes, how secure she is about her height or how into fashion she is. For example, red soles on a shoe have become a clear indication of status as they belong to a famously renown and expensive shoe designer. Jimmy Cho, Kate Spade, Manolo Blahnik, and Vivienne Westwood are names that should roll off the tongue of any true shoe aficionado. Zappos, D.S.W. and Overstock.Com would be bookmarked for quick reference on the laptop of any Imelda Marcos in training. Some would say that shoes make an outfit and the story of Cinderella certainly proved that finding the right shoe can change a girl's life in an instant. A pedicure, brightly painted toes and the perfect pair of sandals are considered the rite of passage to herald the Spring and an end to winter weather in many college dorms across the nation.

The original purpose for shoes was to protect the feet from sharp objects, dirty and dusty roads and from the elements of weather. Their design varied from culture to culture and evolved over time to better fit the lifestyle demands of those who wore them. Specific styles of shoes were developed to aide those with particular occupations or avocations. There are boots for hiking, steel toe work boots, cowboy boots, various athletic shoes, and even specialty shoes for different types of dance. While the first shoes were primarily utilitarian in function; they have evolved into a fashion element often times being nothing more than adornment. Some shoes serve no other purpose than to decorate and to call attention to the feet that wear them.

Many of the shoes popular in today's fashions could be argued as being counterproductive to their original purpose. They were designed to sell but never to seriously be worn for any length of time or to walk any distance. Very high platforms, nail-like spikes, tight and pointed toes, and the use of non-durable fabrics such as silks and velvets make these works of art anything other than utilitarian. These shoes could be referred to as someone's "sitting only shoes" or "Sunday meeting shoes". Wearing these contraptions could actually result in great damage to your feet rather than offer them protection.

While fancier designed shoes were worn within the royal courts as well as for marriage feasts and other festive occasions; the earliest shoes worn in daily life were sandals consisting of little more than a piece of leather or skin tied to the feet with twine or lacing. A specific type of animal skin mentioned in scripture as having been used by God himself to make the sandals for the people of Israel is badger's skin (Ezekiel 16:10). This marine animal's skin was also used as the visible outer covering or fourth layer of curtains for the tabernacle (Exodus 26:1-14). The most remarkable testament to the durability of the shoes that God provides his people is the fact that these shoes did not wear out nor cause the feet to swell or blister while the Children of Israel wandered in the wilderness for forty years (Deuteronomy 8:4, 29:5).

THESE BOOTS ARE MADE FOR BATTLE

Perhaps the sturdiest of all shoes mentioned within Biblical text are the boots of a Roman solider. These were shoes designed not only to endure the long marches of the Roman army but also to be used as brutal and deadly instruments of war. The Roman soldier's shins and calves were carefully covered by knee high boots that were wrapped with sheets of metal which were tightly lashed to the feet and legs and held together with leather thongs and additional bits and pieces of metal. The end result was a very heavy weapon of battle. The sheer weight alone would serve to crush anything that got in an advancing soldier's way. Imagine the noise that an entire Roman Legion would have made as they marched into a territory wearing these heavily armored boots. The ground would have trembled under their weight as they approached from the distance.

Historians suggest that the most important aspect of the Roman soldier's boots were the "hobnails" or spikes that were secured into the soles and the two very sharp spikes that protruded out from the front of each boot's toe box. The spikes in the soles were used in defensive battle or to protect a territory from being overtaken by intruding armies. Every soldier would select his place across the front lines of defense and then securely "dig in" with those spikes. Each warrior would become virtually impossible to push over once those anchors were planted deeply into the ground. The spikes jutting out from the toe of each boot were also used for offensive battle. Soldiers were skilled in using them like daggers or spears to pierce the flesh of any adversary. A line of Roman soldiers could keep right on marching as they high stepped and slashed into the flesh of all horses or humans who dared to run out in opposition to an on-coming battalion.

It might be difficult to imagine anyone referring to such horrific shoes as " shoes of the gospel of peace" yet that is precisely what Paul does in Ephesians 6:14 -15. Paul is speaking of the spiritual battle in which the followers of Christ are now enlisted. He wrote this letter to the Church of Ephesus while he was imprisoned in Rome. I imagine that he had ample access and opportunity to study the pieces of armor worn by his prison guards and the other Roman soldiers who passed by. He probably looked at Roman armor and those boots every day. It makes sense that in instructing the soldiers for the Lord stationed in Ephesus, Paul would simply refer to pieces of armor with which his audience was now quite familiar. In verse eleven (11) Paul tells the New Testament church to put on the entire armor of the Lord to stand against their spiritual enemies. Four more times within the text of Ephesians 6 Paul reminds these Christian warriors that they were going to have to stand against the enemy (Ephesians 6: 11, 13, 14). Standing would seem more possible now knowing that the armor which God had provided included a pair of metal coated, hobnail, spike toe, knee high boots that could be firmly anchored into the ground. These shoes could truly be called "killer boots". Imagine staking a claim and then stomping the enemy's head with these heavy objects strapped tightly to your feet and anchored securely on solid ground!

How then could Paul refer to such instruments of war as "the shoes of peace"? There are two possible applications. The first application would be that when a soldier knows that she has been so sufficiently equipped by the Commander in Chief then she can rest in total peace, secure in her boots, regardless of the war that rages. These killer boots are the shoes that would grant her peace in the midst of the battle because she had a firm foundation. There was no shaking in these boots because they were securely rooted and planted. This soldier was grounded.

The second application would be that while it is true that these boots were instruments of battle, as was all the armor Paul discussed in Ephesians chapter 6; they were also instruments of peace as it was only through the defeat of the enemy that true peace could be established. Just as David had to defeat Goliath in order to silence his taunts, so each soldier of the Lord will have to stand up and quiet the roars of that toothless lion that seeks to defeat her. We cannot leave the battlefield or simply choose not to participate in the battle. There are no conscientious objectors in the Lord's Army. Each fearfully wonderful woman of God must engage in hand to hand combat with her spiritual adversaries at some time or another (Ephesians 6:12). Other times she will fend him off by anchoring in and taking her stand shod in her boots of peace (Ephesians 6:15). Paul said that we would need to be strong in the Lord, put on his whole armor and shod our feet with the preparation of the gospel of peace (Ephesians 6:10, 11, 15). It is in being firmly grounded in the truth of the gospel that we stand against the manipulations and lies of Satan. Our army boots fully cover us as we go out and meet the enemy.

In the Old Testament we read that soldiers and scouts within the Children on Israel's tribes put on their shoes which they had carefully laid aside just inside their door when they prepared for battle or went out on a scouting assignment (Joshua 9:5, 13). Paul reminds us that we must not lay aside the gospel when we go out into the world. We must put on the gospel of Christ to march into the enemy's territory, to enlarge our territory, and to defend what Satan seeks to take from us. We can also march forward and claim what was once enemy territory with our feet covered and protected by these peacemaking, peace bringing shoes that God provides all of his army (Psalm 60:8, 12).

TAKE YOUR SHOES OFF – REST AWHILE.

If a soldier of the Lord must put their shoes on to travel, to go out to meet the enemy, or to march into battle; then when do we take them off? This is certainly the question on many of our minds after a long day of shopping or standing in four inch stilettos. We can't wait to get home, kick back and put up our bare feet. Even the greatest of all shoe lovers must concede that there is a time to run barefoot through the grass or to don the pink fluffy slippers. Likewise, this would be a burning question in the minds of many Roman soldiers after having marched for miles across the arid and rocky land of the region in those killer boots of theirs. When would they get to sit down and rest awhile? When could their tired and aching feet get some relief?

The taking off of shoes was actually significant in many Biblical customs. For example, people removed their shoes in respect and reverence to a holy place (Joshua 5:15). Accordingly, priests officiated barefoot while in the temple. This act could have been performed because most travel was accomplished by foot and on dusty roads hence shoes were unclean and therefore unfit for holy or set apart places. It was also customary to remove one's dusty shoes or sandals when entering into a place to have a meal (Luke 7:38, John 13:5-6). The only exception to this norm would be that sandals were worn during the eating of the Passover meal to symbolize the participants' readiness to quickly follow their God (Exodus 12:11).

It is God who commands Moses to take off his shoes before coming any closer to His presence within the burning bush (Exodus 3:5). The removal of the shoes in this scenario was clearly a sign of reverence for the holy ground upon which Moses would stand, but there may also be some deeper symbolism for God's requirement. Men claimed territory or ownership of property by walking over it with a shod foot (2 Samuel 8:14, Joshua 10:24).The ground upon which God was meeting Moses was holy unto God. That place was not to be walked upon with a shod foot and could not be possessed by Moses or any other man (Buber, (1988). p. 426).

✄ ROADSIDE REFLECTIONS:

- It's just one simple word… "rest"? But how many of us honestly know how to take our shoes off and rest? Is it your tendency to resist the natural rhythm of life complete with ebbs and flows, night and day in the hopes of *getting more done*" or of "squeezing *more sunlight out of the day*"? What do **you** do to relax and to catch a calm and soothing breath? Can you list some of the things that give you comfort, calm, serenity and support when you are stressed, drained, exhausted or dog- tired?

- What does it mean to "rest" spiritually?

Having someone else remove your shoe in public was a sign or disrespect or of humiliation and a loss of dignity for the individual whose feet were bare. Such shoe removal was the recourse for any widowed woman who had a brother in law who refused to take her as a wife in accordance with the Levirate marriage custom of the Jewish people (Deut. 25:9). Perhaps Moses was showing his great humility when this leader of the tribes of Israel willingly removed his shoes and stripped his feet naked under God's direct command.

Taking off one's shoes also indicated an obligation or an oath to fulfill a commitment. This is illustrated in the book of Ruth when Boaz threw off his shoe to signify that he would purchase a piece of land for Naomi and would take Ruth as his wife (Ruth 4:7-8). In this scenario, by removing his shoe Boaz performed an act of redemption on the behalf of another and fulfilled the law of Levirate marriage (Radin, (1948) p.129). It was at the burning bush that God commissioned Moses and sent Him to Pharaoh to redeem His people out of Egypt (Exodus 3:2-15).

WASHING THE DUST FROM YOUR FEET

As we discussed earlier, it was a social norm within the culture of Biblical text to remove one's shoes when coming into a home to share a meal. It was also customary for the owner of the home to offer dinner guests a bowl of water with which to wash the dust from their feet before settling down to share a meal. A wealthy dinner host might offer a servant from the household to wash the feet of the dinner guests. Such foot washing was a widespread practice in the East and was practiced dating back as early as the time of Father Abraham (Gen. 18:4; 19:2). While the practice may have shown honor to a guest who was being received it was also very practical from a hygiene and cleanliness perspective. Folks traveled from place to place either barefoot or in flimsy sandals. They traveled along roads and paths that were either dusty or muddy and manure and debris lined. Their feet would be dirty, smelly and unpleasant by the time they arrived for dinner at someone's home. Washing the feet of a dinner guest was certainly a nice gesture for them but was also considerate for everyone sharing a reclining bench with them around the meal table.

In the thirteenth chapter of the gospel of John, Jesus participates in this social custom. Jesus was now performing the very same act of humiliation and adoration that Mary of Bethany had performed on his feet earlier (John 12:3-11). He is in the upper room of a home preparing to share his last meal with his disciples before his betrayal when he washes their feet. It is interesting to note that He didn't just leave out a bowl and towel so that his disciples might each wash their own feet upon entering the upper room. He didn't commission any of the disciples to perform this act on his behalf, and he didn't ask the owner of the home to provide a household servant. Jesus himself washed each of the disciple's smelly, dirty feet. Remember that they were celebrating the Passover meal together and that this meal was taken with shoes on. This is why he washed their feet at the completion of the meal and not prior (John 13:2). Why did He choose to perform this act at this time and in this manner? There are several lessons that we can gather from Jesus' example and hopefully apply to our own lives.

The first lesson is the most obvious since Jesus spoke it himself. In John 13:14-17 Jesus tells his disciples that if their Lord and teacher could stoop down and wash his followers' feet then they certainly ought to wash one another's feet. His example must have cut them at the very core since none of them had thought to offer this act of kindness either for their Lord or for each other at any time on that night or prior. Imagine their humiliation as Christ took a servant's position at each of their feet and wiped away the filth knowing that they had not offered to wipe away the day's grime from each other. Luke's account of their final meal with Jesus indicates that the disciples were busy bickering over who would be greatest in Jesus' kingdom rather than seeking ways to better love and serve each other (Luke 22:24-33).

Let the self- serving and bickering behavior of his disciples as contrasted against the example that Christ gave remind us that we need to lovingly serve each other and seek to help each other wash off the manure and garbage that we may have trudged through in our daily walk here on earth. We need to love each other deeply, because love covers a multitude of sin (1 Peter 4:8). We also need to encourage each other toward repentance and gently restore one another to fellowship with the Body of Christ (Galatians 6:1). Anyone of us should take caution in passing judgment as we could step into the exact same mud puddle the next time and be in need of the same gentle foot washing from one of our sisters.

We show our greatest strength when we are willing to lower ourselves and to become a servant to those around us; when we are willing to decrease that His presence might increase (John 3:30). Tenderness is a strength that exhibits the power of God's grace and our vulnerability to the needs of others channels His love. Our faith is most strong when we are willing to be weak and lowly, gentle and kind in the lives of others.

Many people seek personal power or positions of esteem without realizing that legitimate power comes from an internally recognized authority and is not contingent upon the impressions of others or on outward appearances. Jesus proved himself most strong when he was willing to be abased, insulted and broken due to His love for others. Jesus placed himself physically on the cross for our behalf and now calls upon us to place ourselves mentally, emotionally and spiritually on the altar and to be willing to be humbled, broken and crushed for others (Matthew 16:24, 1 Corinthians 15:31). The servant of the Lord must be gentle as He was gentle (2 Timothy 2:24). We must deny ourselves and resist the temptation of seeking to promote ourselves if we are ever going to gain a deeper insight into the mind of Christ and the heart of God. Our expectation for reciprocation, recognition or praise for our acts of service and kindness should be sought from God and not of any person. We are required to surrender our very selves to God and submit to one another so that He might be lifted up and glorified (Romans 6:13, Galatians 6:14, John 12:32).

In Jesus' act of physically washing his disciples' feet he sought to provide them with a deeper understanding of what His upcoming crucifixion was about to accomplish for each of them. The spiritual transaction taking place and illustrated through this simple act would go far beyond that of merely washing off surface level dirt and grime that had accumulated on the disciples' feet. In washing each of the disciple's feet, Jesus lovingly and willingly took their filth onto himself. Their dirt literally became part of his clothing. It was transferred from their being unto his. Imagine that towel which he had wrapped around his waist growing more grungy and disgusting with every additional wipe (John 13:4 -5). Their cleanliness cost him his purity.

No one else in that room could spiritually do for those men what Jesus was now seeking to illustrate within the physical. He was offering a picture of the transaction which would occur at the time of his supreme act of sacrifice in going to the cross. His death would take their sin from them just as that towel had taken their dirt. He alone was the only one who could take the sin of the world upon himself (John 1:29, 1 John 3:5). Their salvation cost him his purity and righteousness.

Jesus alludes to the deeper meaning of his actions in John 13:7 when he is speaking to Peter. Peter saw Jesus approaching to wash his feet and became indignant at the thought and vocally rejected Christ's service (John 13:6-8). Jesus told Peter that he could not yet fully understand the true meaning of his actions but that later it would be clear (John 13:7).

Simon Peter was the impetuous and zealous follower of Christ with whom I relate the most. He was willing to launch out into the deep waters with the Lord and impetuously jumped out of the boat to join Jesus for a walk across the water (Luke 5:4, Matthew 14:29-30).When Jesus explained that if Peter would not allow him to wash his feet then Peter could have no part with him, Peter did a total turn around and boisterously commanded the Lord to not only wipe his feet but to give him a head to toe shower (John 13:8-10). Jesus explained that after Peter's feet had been washed and Christ had taken Peter's dirt upon himself then Peter would be clean through and through. He would not ever again need the total cleansing that his Messiah was now offering. Peter had been immersed in the depth of the atonement, drenched with the waters of life and bathed in the springs of forgiveness. Jesus had washed his sin from him with spring of living water. From that point forward all that would be required of him would be their daily bathing and repentance of sin (John 13:10). Jesus confirmed that He was their promised Messiah (John 13:19-20).

We can draw one final lesson from this conversation between the Lord and Peter recorded in John chapter 13. From it we learn a valuable lesson that each of us needs to apply to our daily lives. Even the most careful and most dedicated followers of Jesus will miss a step from time to time. As we travel life's journey we will step into something unaware and sully our feet as a result. When this happens, then just like Peter, we will need to show our dirty feet to Jesus and allow his living water to cleanse us (John 7:37-39). This daily act of humble confession (openly showing the dirt we've stepped in to the Lord) is vital in maintaining a free and intimate relationship with Jesus. Showing him our daily grime allows him the opportunity to forgive us, restore us and then reestablish relationship with us. His healing and forgiving waters are always available to us and ever proceeding freely from God's throne. As we pour out our hearts to God He pours out his grace to us. We put out our water jars and God sends down the cleansing rains for our dry souls (Job 38:34-38).

Confessing our sin openly to the Lord also signifies our cooperation and the obedient surrender of our path to his leading. God is then able to heal that which is broken and to restore beauty to the parched and dry places of our lives. He can use our stumbling and failings for our benefit as well as for benefit in the lives of those around us (Hebrews12:10). We can call upon the Lord in the midst of our troubles , commit the mess we've made to him and trust that he will meet us right where we are, forgive us and deliver us (Joel 2:32). After we confess and he cleanses us we can put our shoes back on and be ready to follow as he leads. With both feet back on the ground, we are now ready to move out into an enlarged territory and an endless realm of possibility (Mark 9:23).

Jesus provided us with wonderful illustrations through his washing of the disciples' feet. He provided a clear picture of what was accomplished on the cross and of what He continues to do for us daily. Jesus literally entered into the Holy of Holies as our sacrifice and offered his own blood as our sin payment (Hebrews 10:14-21). He took our sin upon himself and became our kinsman redeemer. He is now our high priest who intercedes on our behalf. He sprinkles us and washes us with the purest of water when we confess our daily sin to him (Hebrews 10:22). We can come boldly to him and find grace and forgiveness (Hebrews 4:16). Our praise will open up streams of water in the desert places of our lives, and when we bring our empty vessels to our Father he will still supply all our needs according to his riches in glory (Numbers 21:17, Philippians 4:19). He is still the living water and he alone can impart springs of refreshment to flow from our souls into the lives of others (John 4:13-14, John 7:38).

SHAKING THE DUST FROM YOUR FEET

When Jesus called his twelve disciples, he called them to a life that required leaving their homes and being willing to travel long distances by foot down dusty roads (Luke 9: 58). These men, along with the women who joined them, dealt with the elements of weather such as wind, rain and extreme heat. They also had hostile encounters with thieves, wild animals and snakes along their way. As they went with Jesus from place to place, they were dependent upon the hospitality and acceptance of the residents of the various towns for lodging, food and water and for protection against the enraged religious leaders and fearful political groups that were seeking to either stone them, imprison them or to kill them. The New Testament book of Acts records that the first missionaries of the gospel were publically beaten, thrown out of town or had to leave in the middle of the night in fear of their lives. They were ridiculed and rejected, slandered and stoned.

The political unrest within the region in which most of Jesus' travels occurred was mounting. There was growing discontent among the citizens of these Jewish communities. Riots and uprising were on an increase within this Region of the Roman Empire. The Romans were fully aware of Jewish teachings concerning a liberator that would come and free them. Jesus worried governmental officials because they feared that his followers would rise up and lead a revolt against Roman rule. Given the above circumstances, it is easy to understand why Jesus and his followers were not openly and warmly greeted at each new town they visited. He wasn't just feared by Roman political rule but was also viewed as a threat to the religious structure of these communities because he openly challenged and debated with the religious leaders of the time. He publicly disagreed with the Sadducees over their teaching and rebuked the Pharisees for their personal behavior and lifestyles (Luke 20:27-40, Matthew 23:1-4). Jesus greatly offended these religious leaders by speaking what they perceived as blasphemy by considering himself as equal with God (Mark 2:3-12, John 14:7-10).

Unkind rumors were also circulating throughout the region about the behavior of this so called "Messiah" because Jesus chose to meet with Samaritans, demoniacs, and the deaf, blind and diseased; all of whom were known as sinners. How could any true Messiah choose to keep company with known sinners rather than to gather with the pious and religious law abiding Sadducees and Pharisees? As a result of his social interaction, Jesus was labeled as a drunk and a glutton who openly broke temple rules and was charged with keeping the company of people of ill repute, such as tax collectors, prostitutes and others of society's outcasts.

It was under these conditions and within this stressful set of circumstances that Jesus sent his followers out "like sheep to the slaughter" (Romans 8:36) and instructed them that if the people of a town would not welcome them or listen to their words they were to "shake the dust from their feet" when they left (Matthew 10:14-15). This action was physically performed as an act of protest against that town and as sign of God's impending judgment upon the people residing there. According to Jewish custom, shaking the dust from one's feet symbolized separation from the people residing in the town or place from which the dust originated. The disciples shook the dust from their feet to separate themselves from those who had chosen to reject their Messiah and his message. In essence, these disciples were saying that they would not be held accountable for the actions of this town when God sent his judgment upon them. Their slate was wiped clean.

By shaking the dust from their feet, the disciples were free to leave in peace, knowing that they had done all within their power to reach those hard hearted people. They were also leaving behind all the insults, accusations and biting comments that might have been hurled against them. The dust and dirt of that town was not going to occupy even the smallest amount of space on their bodies nor would it be allowed to enter into their spirits. That dirt was going no further. They weren't carrying it with them. The disciples were making a clean start on a new adventure. They were shaking it off and moving ahead.

AVOIDING PITFALLS AND POTHOLES

Hopefully we have now ascertained that conflict is not unchristian and that conflict is going to happen (2 Timothy 3:12). Sooner or later something or someone is going to scuff up the toes of our favorite shoes; and it is impossible to live out an entire life here on earth without eventually rubbing someone the wrong way. The seasoned traveler has learned that nothing is gained through conflict avoidance. Friendships are not maintained by ignoring something that is bothering us or by burying our feelings. Conflict avoidance is not conflict resolution. Ignoring a problem will not make it go away any better than closing our eyes while playing hide and seek will keep others from seeing us. Sooner or later our problems have a way of finding us or of catching up to us.

If it is a given that conflict is going to happen along life's pathways then the development of positive conflict resolution skills will provide vital tools for all ambassadors. Resolving conflict tactfully can be the passageway to peacemaking and the corridor to greater communication. Learning how to approach conflict truthfully, confidently and carefully will deeper the levels of communication within our interpersonal relationships. This will increase unity within the Body of Christ and provide greater understanding for those who are not believers. As ambassadors for Christ we need to be tactful. We need to treat other human beings with respect as God's unique creation. As such, we want our speech to be persuasive and passionate but we should never seek to manipulate, threaten, frighten or to cajole another person into accepting Christ or into seeing things from our perspective.

Jesus warned us that being sent out as ambassadors for God's kingdom means that we will sometimes offend others (Matthew 5:11, Luke 12:53). Speaking the truth in love (Ephesians 4:15) will often incite anger or incense a heated response from others. We must remember that some of the people with whom we will interact may have had a previous negative experience with someone claiming to be a Christian. There may be a great deal of misunderstanding or fear that is now fueling their heated response, negativity or debate with us. We will need to be cautious in our expression of zeal and passion for the truth of Jesus to avoid our words from being perceived as judgmental, condescending or angry. Skilled ambassadors will develop the fine balance between assertiveness and sensitivity to the feelings of others.

If we are going to reach others for the kingdom of God, then we must be willing to extend ourselves beyond our comfort levels. We must learn to practice grace and to exercise our tongues with constraint and control even when under great pressure to defend ourselves. Being an ambassador will often require a willingness to be vulnerable to negative reactions such as misunderstanding, hurt feelings, anger and rejection. Peacemakers must sometimes grapple with the mire of human fears and emotions to reach the real issues fueling a conflict. We must ask the Lord to teach us serenity and the power of stillness while in the midst of calamity and turmoil. If we learn anything from the examples drawn from Jesus' life, it is that when we sincerely care we will risk vulnerability and personal emotional upset for the sake of others whom He loves. Following his example, will require that we become broken bread and poured out wine for his lost sheep (Mark 14:22-25). Being willing to reveal our vulnerability will become part of our strength.

Jesus was never afraid to speak truth or to confront a lie when someone's well-being was at stake but He presented the truth in a loving manner and left the decision to accept or to reject that truth with the individual to whom he was speaking. Some people will choose to reject the truth that we offer them. A few of those will go away angry. Others will leave to contemplate further or to mull over the gravity of about what was said. Still others, like the rich young ruler, will go away troubled or saddened because they are unwilling to make the life changes required of them (Luke 18:18-23). Shaking the dust from our feet requires learning to present the truth in love and to leave the results for that presentation up to the Holy Spirit. God promised that His Word does not return void or without accomplishing its purpose (Isaiah 55:11).

AVOIDING SNAKE BITE

The early followers of Jesus encountered thieves, wild animals such as wolves and boars, and venomous snakes as they traveled down those dusty roads from town to town sharing the good news of the gospel (Psalm 80:13, Matthew 10:16) . Because these women were not wealthy or of an upper level socio-economic class, they would have often been barefoot as they traveled. Those who did have the benefit of shoes would have owned flimsy sandals that offered very little protection from snake fangs or animal claws. Of course, the best way for these followers of Jesus to prevent animal attack or snake bite would have been to avoid the places where such beasts lived and would most likely have been encountered. That wasn't always possible as these animals often hid out in the brush and debris or among the rocks away from clear visibility.

Recorded in Acts 28: 1-9 is the story of Paul's encounter with a venomous snake that was peacefully sleeping curled up deep inside a bundle of sticks. Paul had collected those sticks to make a fire for himself and for the other chilly survivors who had been shipwrecked in a storm. The heat generated by the fire that was now consuming the snake's habitat awakened the viper and he clasped onto Paul's hand with his venomous fangs (Acts 28:3-4).The other marooned passengers looked on waiting for Paul's hand to swell or for him to fall over sick and dying from the snake's deadly bite (Acts 28:6). After a reasonable amount of time had passed, the men traveling with Paul realized that their anticipated reaction to the snake bite was not taking place inside Paul. Paul simply shook off the viper into the fire he had built and went on about his business (Acts 28:5). The snake's deadly bite brought Paul no harm.

In addition to shaking the dust from our feet, we must learn to immediately shake off the snake that may have taken hold of our hand and is now seeking to poison us. Often times the fire of our passion and zeal for the truth of God will awaken vipers that have been peacefully sleeping deep inside the souls and spirits of those whom we encounter along our journey. That snake will spit biting remarks and seek to place the venom of offense within our spirit. As ambassadors we must shake off those remarks before that venom has a chance to poison our attitude and our emotions. If the poison is allowed to penetrate our thoughts and our spirit it will cause a reaction within us that will display anything but an attitude that reflects Jesus. While it is true that we do not always have the option of choosing not to be bitten; we can choose how we will react to the bite.

The secret to surviving snake bite lies in learning how to allow others to express their feelings and thoughts freely without taking offense. We must prevent a perceived wrong or negative reaction from another from taking hold of our emotions, entering our thought life and crimpling us. We cannot allow the reactions of others to infiltrate our attitude and direct our subsequent reactions. We must shake it off and go on. Ambassadors on assignment do not waste precious time replaying hurtful scenarios, revisiting negative feelings, or inviting others to take sides or to attend their pity parties. They do not hold grudges or fantasize revenge. Ambassadors filter their thoughts through the mind of Christ and cast down their imaginations to bring every thought in line with kingdom principles (2 Corinthians 10:5). The priorities of the kingdom must take precedent over our personal anger or hurt. We can take our hurts to the Lord and then ask him to heal us and to fill us with his love toward the person who has inflicted our pain.

As ambassadors we must learn to take our offenses to God rather than to others. We must hold our tongue, be voiceless and not grumble or complain to others or about others. Remember, often time our silence can be far more eloquent that a speech especially when in a time of wrongful accusation or difficulty. Jesus showed his strength by holding his tongue (Matthew 15:23). He is peace and he promises to give peace. In our quietness and confidence is our strength. We must ask Jesus to be the source of our peace and help us stay aligned to his teaching. Our emotions will betray us when we are feeling hurt or unjustly accused. Being still and allowing Him to be God in a situation often includes holding our tongues still.

Fearfully wonderful women of God cannot seek vindication or retaliation through gossip or slander when being attacked or treated unkindly (Romans 12:19). Followers of Christ temper their reactions by remembering that God requires us to forgive others just as he has forgiven us (Colossians3:13) and that He will forgive us as we have forgiven others (Matthew 6:14-15). It is for the sake of Christ's grace towards us that we need to give grace to others.

God's word is very clear regarding our need to forgive. Learning not to carry an offense is for our benefit, growth and protection. The poison of unforgiveness or bitterness compromises our testimony, our daily walk and our relationship with our Father. Followers of Christ are warned in Mark 11: 25 that God will not hear our prayers until we go handle unresolved feelings and offenses that we may have with our sisters. We are told to stop praying and to go handle the offense and then return to pray. We can see from this scripture passage that forgiveness of another is for the benefit of the person seeking to interact with God through prayer. Making things right with someone else or acting in selfless forgiveness releases us from the poisonous effects that result in negative thoughts, bitter attitudes and critical spirits. Simply stated, learning to forgive prevents sin and allows us to openly communicate with God to receive the comfort, grace and healing that we need. Forgiveness is a choice enacted by our will and transacted in our spirits. We may not feel like forgiving another person but the act of forgiving actually empowers us because it frees us from them having any power over our feelings, thoughts or attitude. Choosing to forgive and to believe that God will handle the situation holds us steady in our walk and strengthens our relationship with God.

※ ROADSIDE REFLECTIONS:

- How do you relate to the idea of comparing taking offense with another to being snake bit? What scriptures do you carry in your first-aid kit to aid you when someone has attempted to inflict pain or to poison you with their venomous words? How do you shake it off and respond to such attacks in love?

- Is there dust from past experiences that you need to shake off before you can move further along on your journey with the Lord?

FEARFULLY FABULOUS FOOTWEAR

How could anyone possibly think that the dusty, calloused, cracked and aching feet of those men and women who traveled for the gospel of Jesus were beautiful? Traveling long distances in sandals would hardly contribute to feet that were soft, smooth and well pedicured. The feet of Junia or those of Tryphena and Tryphosa were not the sort of feet that would grace the pages of a fashion magazine or be found in a shoe designer's advertisement. Yet in Romans 10:15 we read: *"How beautiful are the feet of those who bring good news"*.

Have you ever meet anyone who wasn't willing to listen to a little good news? In the midst of life's trials and tribulations we all long for some word of hope or comfort. A joke or a quick laugh is always a welcome lift for our heavy hearts and spirits. The feet of ambassadors are beautiful because they bring the good news and exceeding joy of a hope and a future. The good news we share tells of how anyone can be acquitted on the Day of Judgment. It shares the key to being found righteous through faith in Christ Jesus. Our words show lost and lonely souls the path to an open relationship with their Abba- Father. There is an infinite significance and an everlasting value in the gospel that we share. Our message is life changing.

As ambassadors of God's kingdom we are heroines. We come offering life to the dying, hope to the hopeless and freedom to the imprisoned. Our good news offers an eternity of blessing that is infinitely better than anything this temporal life on earth can offer. Our Lord has commissioned us to "preach good news to the poor". He has sent us to "bind up the brokenhearted, to proclaim freedom for the captives and the release from darkness for the prisoners" (Isaiah 61:6).

What then should be the footwear of heroines who, in the face of ridicule, rebuke, adversity and rejection go forth from a position of humility and brokenness to bring this message of grace and life to the dying and desperate? Should God's wonderful women wear steel toe boots, fireman's boots, Army boots, or the cloth covered shoes of the skilled surgeon? Our assignment may require all of these as we are engaging in battle, binding up wounds, freeing our enemy's prisoners and rescuing souls from the fire of self-destruction. We may also wish to pack bridal shoes and ballet slippers as we are the invited guests at the marriage feast of the lamb and will dance for joy when Christ returns to claim us, as well as in victory at the defeat of our enemy, and in worship before the throne of God (1 Samuel 18:6-7, Jeremiah 31:4, Psalm 150:4 , Revelation 19:4-10). If we glance into our shoe bag we see that our Lord is sending us out on our journey well prepared with our feet perfectly shod. He is outfitting our feet just as he did the Children of Israel, the missionary Peter and all those ambassadors who walked with him before us:

> *Then the angel said to him, "Put on your clothes and sandals." And Peter did so. "Wrap your cloak around you and follow me," the angel told him- Acts 12:8*

> *You, who bring good tidings to Zion, go up on a high mountain. You, who bring good tidings to Jerusalem, lift up your voice with a shout, lift it up, and do not be afraid; say to the towns of Judah, "Here is your God!" Isaiah 40:*

CHAPTER 8

The Accessories Wrap

While accessories are not the mainstay of a woman's wardrobe, if used correctly, they do have the power to make a wardrobe unique, to take an outfit up a notch, or to bring a mundane set of clothing to life. After all, clothes are inanimate objects void of any life or movement until the spirit and energy of a person brings them animation. The value of accessories is their capacity to fold into our wardrobe seamlessly and to enhance or enrich our total look. For example, we could take the same exact little black dress and pair of heels, finish them off with different accessories, and discover two or three radically distinct silhouettes or fashion statements. The accessories are the finishing touches that complete the distinct fashion statements. They add the life and the dynamic to the clothing on our backs. Accessories are the proverbial icing on the cake, the little added panache or pizzazz that makes a look uniquely ours.

Fashion accessories can range from the classic looks of pearls and gloves to the quirky and trendy fashions that seem to come and go over night. Women who have developed their own sense of style know that the utility, adaptability, versatility and longevity of the accessory must be considered in addition to its immediate appeal if it is going to be an item of true value. Because we are seeking to pack lightly, we must be extra diligent in the consideration of each accessory that we will include in our wrap. Those accessories that will truly be winning touches will be the ones that have lasting charm, can be worn with several different items in our wardrobe, and that will stand up to scrutiny from season to season. Any woman can follow a fashion trend by throwing on a bracelet, a belt, or a string of pearls; but the secret to utilizing accessories correctly is in learning to develop one's own personal style or in becoming one's own style icon.

OUTGROWING SPIRITUAL CHARM BRACELETS

Charm bracelets are an accessory that has come in and out of vogue; but at one time they were quite popular to wear and to share with friends. Many of us may still have our charm bracelet packed away in a box or in the back of our jewelry chest. Every girl who owned a bracelet would collect tokens or trinkets to add to it over time. Girls would compare the number of charms and the contents of one another's bracelets in the halls of school or at slumber parties. There were charms that signified membership in clubs or organizations such as the band, student government, a sports team, or the cheerleading squad. There were charms to mark accomplishments such as perfect attendance, honor roll achievement and graduation from junior high or high school. Charms were also given for special occasions such as for birthdays and at Christmas. If a woman continued her collection she might even have a charm marking the birth of each of her children. Bragging rights came to the girl who had either the highest number of charms on her bracelet or who wore the bracelet that carried those charms indicating elite status, enviable position or some other prestige.

Sadly many women within the body of Christ approach their spiritual life in much the same manner as they would a charm bracelet. They join a women's circle, sing in the choir, attend a discipleship class and memorize scripture all in an effort to achieve another charm to place on their spiritual bracelet. They've learned the lingo, attended the meetings, read the spiritual growth book of the moment, and know the names of all the popular speakers leading women's conferences or currently available on disc.

A charm bracelet approach to spirituality can be equated to putting on a show or to developing our spiritual life in the hopes of impressing someone else or in gaining access to a particular group of women. While we never really wear a tangible bracelet into our spiritual gatherings we present a false spiritualty or put our holiness on display for others to inspect and to approve. We seek spiritual adoration, acceptance and the praise of others for our accomplishments, dedication and ministry. We want to belong to the right organizations, know the right interpretations of scripture and follow the right church doctrine or disciplines. We are going through the ritual and the routine but have developed a form of religion with no power there in (2 Timothy 3:5). Rather than compare our walk and our growth to our true standard, Jesus Christ (Matthew 28:18-20, Ephesians 5:23-24), we compare our walk to those around us just as we compared our charms on our bracelets.

The charm bracelet mentality of spirituality is not always easy to discern. It may not be overt or even a behavior of which a person is aware. An individual may be very sincere in their desire to live a godly life and in their pursuit of spiritual growth and fellowship may fall into this mentality. Churches and organizations may even encourage it unaware with their endless training classes and programs. Rather than relying upon the Holy Spirit to guide our footsteps or to lead us in ministry we may feel guilted into getting busy or compelled to join a class out of a need to please or to impress church leadership. This mentality of comparing our spiritual walk and achievements to others often leaves the women of God exhausted, empty and thirsting for freshness in their relationships with others and with their creator. We may also develop insecurities, jealousies or fan clubs within our groups if one woman is perceived to be the one who "has it all" spiritually while others are striving to emulate or copy her.

The charm bracelet mentality will stagnate our uniqueness as individual women and retard our growth and development of our own spiritual gifts and talents. Group think may also develop if our desire to belong becomes so strong that we fail to challenge one another or to share new insights or varying opinions. We cease to be iron sharpening iron (Proverbs 27:17) if we devolve into an amen club or a chorus of agreement.

The time has come for fearfully wonderfully women to put away their spiritual charm bracelets. As individual members of the body of Christ we should encourage one another to discover, develop, and freely use our own spiritual gifts and to find our unique ministry within the church. We need to each become our own style icon and to stop trying to look just like everyone else. Since God knows which niche or position He desires for us to fill we should trust Him to shape us and mold us for that unique purpose. God created us as unique individuals. He fashioned our inner most parts complete with passions, creative ideas, personality, and a desire to serve him (Psalm 139:13). He will impart wisdom to the secret chambers of our being if we will only ask Him (Job 38:36, Psalm 51:6). We need to let his wisdom and the mind of Christ ultimately influence our decisions, not a spiritual growth book, not a church leader, not even a best friend.

PERSONALIZING YOUR STYLE: DISCOVERING YOUR GIFTS AND TALENTS

As God's fearfully wonderful women we have all been entrusted with spiritual gifts and talents. The purpose of these gifts is to use them to carry out the work of the kingdom of God and to increase his presence or enlarge his territory here on earth. They are not to be put on display or to be used for personal gain or praise. Our use of God's gifts must come with the recognition that they are HIS gifts which he has gifted to us so that we might in turn gift others. Spiritual gifts are to be used to encourage, to teach, and to minister love to others with whom we share our journey (1Corinthians 12:4, Ephesians 4:7). When we travel together each of us employs our spiritual gifts and our talents to help our sisters in developing a stronger walk, a clearer path, or steadier footsteps.

We are all gifted differently and must learn how to serve in a way that best expresses our unique gifts, talents and natural inclinations. What purpose would there be in all of the companions sharing a journey having identical gifts, strengths and limitations? How would they benefit each other or add strength to the corporate group? A tea service is only complete when there is a pitcher, a sugar bowl, a creamer and a cup and saucer out on the table. Each piece serves a distinct and vital part in the whole. What hostess sets a table with two pitchers and no tea cup? So it is with spiritual gifts. God places a variety of gifts in each grouping of his ambassadors. Our spiritual gifts are not just to benefit our independent relationship with the Lord. We are also responsible for discovering our spiritual gifts and for using them in service to all the members of God's Kingdom.

Discovering our spiritual gifts is about becoming who God designed us to be. For some of us the process of becoming who God designed us to be may take a longer period of time than for others. One thing is certain, and that is that when we do discover who we really are in God's perfect plan we will experience a freedom and a fullness of life as never before. That is because our life is now being energized with the exhaustless energy of the Holy Spirit as we rely upon him to lead us and show us our individual assignments and distinct purpose within the kingdom (Acts 1:8). It feels so wonderful to discover our unique gifts or purpose as ambassadors for the kingdom of God. We feel our best when we are operating as God designed us to operate. This might sound superficial, but it isn't. Discovering and using our spiritual gifts is about being confident and knowing who we are in Christ Jesus. Each fearfully wonderful woman of God serves in a distinct and vital way to the ministry of the whole; whether she cooks a meal, teaches a class, sings in the choir, keeps the nursery, does the daily chores for a friend who is in the hospital, or organizes a church rummage sale for missions. No task or position is of greater importance than another. Each of us is making a valuable contribution to the work of God's kingdom. Each of us matters to the Lord and to the Body of Christ.

Once a spiritual gift has been discerned, it is the responsibility of each ambassador to develop and to use her gifts in tangible ways. After all, a gift is of no value unless it is offered up in service to others and in worship to our Lord. We must not be shy in using our spiritual gifts or in encouraging others to exercise theirs. Also, we must not assume that each of us will only receive one spiritual gift to last our life time. God distributes spiritual gifts as the body has need. An ambassador may move in one gifting in a given situation and then develop a new gift or move in a totally different gifting due to a new set of circumstances. As fearfully wonderful women of God we need to open to receive any and all gifts that our Father wishes to bestow upon us. He may choose to do something completely new with us as we move in and out of the seasons of our lives. Our greatest fulfillment in life will come when we are open to seeing his strong hand in everything that He presents to us and then trust him to stretch us and to use us in incredible ways that reach far beyond human possibility. With God nothing is impossible (Luke 1:37). He speaks of the unseen as if it is already occurring (Hebrews 4:12). God can take our ordinary lives and meager talents and do mighty things in us and through us if we will only believe (Jeremiah 33:3, John 14:12).

A final word of caution to consider regarding spiritual gifts is that many ambassadors have shared that their area of gifting seems to also be their Achilles' heel, their greatest vulnerability, or greatest area of downfall and temptation toward sin. For example, many people operating in gifts that primarily involve their tongue such as teaching or inspirational speaking have shared that sins of the tongue are an area in which they falter. They confess difficulty with embellishing the truth, overstating the facts or some other misuse of their tongue. Those with musical gifting often struggle with pride or arrogance while counselors and ministers have shared their need be cautious of infatuations, gossip and sexual temptations. It seems that the principal target for our enemy is often the very core of our ministry or the heart of that which is consecrated or ordained for God's service. Nothing can be more destructive to our calling or more devastating to the work of the Lord than for us to use our gifting to gain influence, approval of others or authority that is not God given. We will be vulnerable to the traps and snares of the enemy if we do not recognize our weaknesses and stay ever vigilant against Satan's schemes. Our gifts must always be under God's control and used for His glory alone. That which He has entrusted to our care can be taken from us if we are not careful to use it properly.

❈ ROADSIDE REFLECTION:

- Do you know your spiritual gifts? How are you using them within the Body of Christ and to further His Kingdom?

- Are you aware of the aspects of your personality, ministry or talents that are most vulnerable to sin and to temptation?

ACCESSORIZING WITH PEARLS

Pearls and elegance go hand in hand. A string of pearls is synonymous with a classic fashion statement and for many centuries the word pearl has become a metaphor for something very rare, precious, or of high value. The most valuable pearls occur spontaneously within oysters and other bi-valves living in the wild. These are extremely rare finds and are often well beyond the budget constraints of most women. For this reason, man-made, farmed or cultured pearls have been created and are more widely available within a range of price points. Pearls now come in a variety of shapes, sizes and colors and are being worn by today's fashion icons with everything from ball gowns to blue jeans. They have an undeniable appeal and are desired by women of all ages and stations in life. Whether we are discussing a woman of mature elegance such as former First lady Barbara Bush or a younger lady just beginning to build her jewelry case, pearls must be included in the complete accessory wardrobe.

HOW PEARLS ARE MADE

"But we have this treasure in earthen vessels that the excellency of the power may be of God, and not of us." II. CORINTHIANS 4:5.

The formation of a natural pearl begins when a foreign substance slips into the oyster between the mantle and the shell. The oyster's natural reaction is to pad or cover the irritating substance in an effort to protect the animal's soft and sensitive body. The oyster knows that its soft body cannot endure the intrusion of a hard object without this protective layer. It will likely die without this covering. The oyster begins producing layers of protection consisting of the same substance that makes up its hard outer shell. These layers of protection eventually form a pearl. A pearl is literally an irritating substance that has been padded with layer upon layer of protection. Cultured pearls are created by the same process as natural pearls, but pearl farmers give the oysters a little nudge by artificially introducing the irritant into a slit made in the tissue of the unsuspecting oyster.

The iridescence that a pearl displays is caused by the multiple overlapping of each successive layer that the animal produces to surround the irritant. The multiple layers break up the light falling on the entire padded surface. The unique luster of each individual pearl depends upon the amount of reflection and diffraction of light that takes place within these translucent layers.

Each fearfully wonderful woman of God has strands of pearls that the Lord has given us to adorn ourselves. These pearls are developed when we allow the grace of God and his healing mercies to cover an offense, or a difficult or trying time in our life. Much like the oyster, we must realize that we are helpless in our present situation and call on God's grace to cover us and to protect us. This is a hard lesson to learn or to accept, but we must learn that it's only when we confess that we are weak that God can work through us. When we embrace our limitations and rely upon God's strength to overcome our trials and tribulations, then God's strength becomes our strength. If we allow his grace to be sufficient and rest in his loving care during times of trial and tribulation, He will produce within us a memory stone in the form of a precious pearl. This pearl will serve to remind us of a time when what the enemy meant for bad was used by God for our good and for His glory (Genesis 50:20, Romans 8:28). It is when we allow his light to be reflected in us during life's trials and tribulations then we shine with an inner beauty and luminescence rivaling the most precious of all pearls.

Pearls are fragile gems. Unlike diamonds and other harder gemstones, they can damage easily. Anyone wishing for the pearls in her accessory case to last will need to take good care of them. Actually, the best thing an ambassador can do for her pearls, besides keeping them away from the harsh chemicals found in perfume or soaps, is to wear them as often as possible. Pearls gain luster and strength when they are exposed to the moisture of our natural body oils. Wearing them daily against our skin will enhance their natural beauty. Wearing our pearls will enhance our faith as well. As we go through life, there will be days when the emotional and physical trials seem too great for us to handle. Gently stroking the pearls that our Lord has lovingly placed around our necks will remind us of the words of Jesus when he said: *"In the world you will have tribulation; but be of good cheer, I have overcome the world"* (John 16:33). The longer an ambassador walks with the Lord the greater the numbers of strands or the larger the size of the pearls that will lovingly adorn her neck. She will radiate with a luster and beauty that will make it evident to all that she has been walking with the Lord (Exodus 34:35). This will particularly be the case if she is willing to offer up her former failures and past forgiven sins for the Lord's ministry and use.

Wearing our adornment of pearls will also be a testimony of encouragement for others. When our sisters who are going through difficulties in their own lives can see the "pearls of great price" that the Lord's grace has produced within us they will gain courage, hope and faith to endure their own circumstances. Everyone's faith will go through tests that will come in various forms and at diverse times (1 Peter 4:12-13). Hearing the testimony of someone who has successfully gone through similar life experiences can be a gentle encouragement and a source of strength from which we can draw. In Hebrews 3:13 we are instructed to "*encourage one another daily*" to avoid being hardened by life's difficulties and then falling into sin. Likewise in Galatians 6:2 we are told: "*Carry each other's burdens, and in this way you will fulfill the law of Christ.*" Of course, Christ sums up precisely what the law is in his words recorded in Matthew 7:12:

> *"So in everything, do to others what you would have them do to you, for this sums up the Law and the Prophets."*

ROADSIDE REFLECTIONS:

- Do you recall personal times of discouragement or great difficulty that God has now made into pearls of adornment in our life? How are you using your pearls' beauty as a testimony to others?
- Perhaps you are holding on to resentment or bitterness from those painful past experiences that God wants you to allow him to cover with his grace and make into something beautiful.

Casting Our Pearls Before Swine

In the seventh chapter of the book of Matthew in a section of the Lord's sermon on the mount Jesus is instructing his followers regarding judging others and on holy living. In verse 6 of this discourse he tells his followers not to give what is holy to dogs or to "cast their pearls before swine". It is interesting that Jesus chooses to use a pig as the unappreciative animal in this parable. Pigs are not kosher or are unclean animals under Jewish law (Leviticus 11:7-8, Deuteronomy 14:8). Jews were forbidden to eat them or to touch their dead carcasses. Clearly, Jesus is referring to those who are outside of the kingdom of God in this illustration.

Jesus implies in this teaching that things that are precious to us as followers, such as our pearls of adornment, should not be placed before people (or pigs) who will not appreciate their value or beauty. Not only does He warn that these people will trample what we hold precious under foot destroying and soiling it but He even goes so far as to warn that these unappreciative swine may turn on us and try to do us bodily harm (Matthew 7:6).

As ambassadors of God in a strange land we need to recognize that we may be criticized when we try to serve God. We may even be persecuted for our faith. We need to have wisdom and discernment as we interact with those who do not share our belief set. We don't need to take off our pearls or hide our faith, but we do need to know when the Holy Spirit is leading us to share and when we need to keep silent. We will need to determine when to offer the pearls of God and when not to do so. Matthew 10:16 cautions us to be aware that as followers of Christ we are like *"sheep among wolves"*. The verse goes on to caution that because this world is not our home and does not share our values we will need to be *"shrewd as serpents, and innocent as doves."* (Matthew 10:16).

Our pearls are precious to us. They are meant to be worn close to our hearts to be shared as the Lord leads. Sometimes merely wearing them as we go about our daily life will be enough for the Lord to radiate through us and for others to see that we are different. Some people will appreciate the difference that the Lord has made in our behavior, attitude and world views. Others will be offended, frightened or possibly even angered by our values and norms. We can do nothing to soften the hardened hearts of such people. We must rely upon the gentle leading of the Holy Spirit to make them open and receptive to the message of the gospel (John 6:44). We are the Lord's messengers. We bring the message of the gospel. The Holy spirit alone can produce the yield or response within another person's heart.

Words do not always have to be exchanged in order for Christ's ambassadors to share the gospel. In many situations the best way to display our testimony for the Lord will be through our actions and our daily behavior. This is particularly true in a work environment or other such place that is hostile to "religious people" or to "proselytizing". In these non-receptive atmospheres our sincere actions can speak a thousand words and be much more effective than rehearsed speeches or loud rebukes. Romans 12:20 tells us that if our enemy is hungry then we should feed him and if they are thirsty, then as followers of our Lord, we should give them something to drink. If we are willing to do such things in honor to the Lord without the expectation of praise or reciprocation, then our enemies will have no argument against the grace and unconditional love of Jesus Christ being displayed. Jesus demonstrated that often times the physical needs and hurts of people have to be calmed before they will be willing to consider their deeper spiritual needs that may have caused the life circumstances in which they presently find themselves. He fed the hungry, healed the sick and bound up the wounds of the afflicted before He shared the way of salvation (Mark 8:1-9, Luke 4:34-37, John 4:43-54).

It is also important to remember as ambassadors of God's kingdom that often this world holds us to a higher standard. Those who do not know Jesus or who may have been hurt by religiosity or legalistic dogma in the past will watch our actions and wait for us to slip up so that they might point to our hypocritical behavior and hold God in contempt. We must be careful to live out our faith without compromise and to use our faith as the foundation for our behavior in the marketplace, in our politics, and in our daily interaction with those around us. Everything that we do must be seasoned with grace and love (Colossians 4:6).We must be careful to truly practice what we profess to believe and to follow our values in all that we say and do (Matthew 5:16). Sometimes people say they value something but their actions say otherwise.

Any woman who wishes to impress on the job will pay close attention to the little details of her attire along with establishing her own personal statement pieces. Ambassadors who are employed within the corporate sector cannot take shortcuts at work such as coming in late, taking an extra- long lunch break or leaving early on Fridays. If we are going to make a difference in present day society then we must strive for excellence (1 Peter 1:16). As followers of Christ we are called to go the extra mile for those whom Christ loves (Luke 6:27-29). We cannot lie on the phone, cheat on our taxes or take care of personal business while on the corporate clock. Engaging in office gossip, borrowing office supplies and fudging on our expense accounts are not acceptable behaviors for ambassadors of God. All these behaviors will bring dishonor to the Lord and damage our testimony (Mark 12:17). We must remember that we are living on a spiritual battlefield and have an enemy that is always looking for any opportunity to tarnish our reputation and to cast doubt on the sincerity of God's promised hope for redemption. If we are the salt of the earth and the light on the hill and our behavior is no different than the masses then what hope of redemption and chance for salvation do we offer to them (Matthew 5:13-16)? Some people will be difficult for us to naturally love. We may feel attacked by their remarks and as if they have trampled all that we hold sacred under their feet with their ridicule or unkind behavior. It is when we are dealing with these people that we will rely upon the love of Christ to radiate through us and to reflect in all that we say and do (Exodus 34:35, 2 Corinthians 3:13). Remember, those who came before us were persecuted for the sake of the gospel as well (Matthew 5:11-12). Allow God's grace to be sufficient in your life so that He can make a cherished pearl out of those unpleasant and trying situations in which you find yourself .

A watch or Time piece

God's plan requires God's timing. Every ambassador of God's kingdom needs a reliable time piece that has been synchronized with our Commander in Chief. This will be an important wardrobe accessory to have if we are going to move strictly under his leading while carrying out his mission on earth. Because our God is "the Eternal God (Deuteronomy 33:27) and "the everlasting God" (Isaiah 40:28) He is not bound to time as we are bound to time. We are so conscious of passing minutes and hours that soon become days and weeks, months and years. These time increments have no meaning to God. He is the great "I am" with no beginning and no end (Exodus 3:14, Isaiah 43:10). He is never hurried, impatient, frantic or late. He is infinite while we are finite. His ways are not our ways and his thoughts are unlike our thoughts (Isaiah 55:8). These attributes of God that should speak to the assurance of His steadfast unwavering dependability can become frustrating for any ambassador who has not surrendered her time and her schedule to the Lord's keeping. Often times we will miss his subtle movement or gentle voice if we are not carefully paying attention. Likewise we may become impatient or disheartened if we feel that He is moving too slowly.

God's timing is based upon another kingdom's set of facts, view of the circumstances and ideas about time constraints. Loyal ambassadors must allow their time clocks to be set to this new disposition. We must be assured that waiting on the Lord is not in vain and that each passing minute has a purpose in God's plan. Ambassadors need to be ever vigilant, ever aware and ever ready to move on God's command. They must also be willing to stop moving altogether and to wait for the call to pick up our belongings and to move out again. In short, ambassadors must go with God or stay put.

While we are at rest, we must also be careful not to become complacent or too comfortable at the rest stop. Way stations are not intended as final destinations and we cannot pitch a tent and set up camp in the middle of the road. Rest stops and way stations provide us with an opportunity to be still and to wait for God to accomplish something beyond our view and of which we are not aware. God will bring to pass exactly what He promised (Acts 27:25). We must remember that have only a partial viewing of God's dealings and actions. Our call to waiting may be very difficult for some of us, but it makes much more sense and expends far less energy than to keep walking aimlessly hoping that we will stumble onto God's purpose and plan. God has a purpose in what appears to be a hold up or a delay. All of our steps are ordered by him (Psalm 37:23). Our time for resting is in his plans. Pieces of pottery rest between firings. Musical instruments rest between notes. God rested from all that He had created (Genesis 2:2). Waiting on the Lord will prevent missteps and take us to our appointed place much more quickly than striking out on our own without a chart or a compass.

Our time is in His hands and soon our captain will give a command for us to follow Him home. We each have only an appointed number of days, weeks, months and years upon this earth; and each of us have the same number of hours in our day in which to serve the Lord and to honor his name (Psalm 39:4). We want to be good stewards of our days here on earth and to redeem our time wisely (Ephesians5:15-16). We can do nothing about yesterday after it has passed and we are not promised a tomorrow. We must make the good use of today's hours a priority before they are too quickly passed. No man knows the hour in which Jesus will return to gather his own (Matthew 24:36). We wait in anticipation for something that we feel is still far off when actually it may be very close at hand; perhaps even with the dawn of tomorrow. As his fearfully wonderful women we want him to find us faithfully taking care of his business when he comes to take us home (Luke 18:8, 1 Thessalonians 5:17). We have a promise that our Father will add length to the lives of all those who follow his commands and keep his statutes (1 Kings 3:14). Committing our days to his keeping and pacing our walk with his time piece will help us be more obedient to his will.

✳ ROADSIDE REFLECTIONS:

- How well do you keep your pace of life synchronized with the Father?

OUR PURSE

Purses are usually the accessory upon which women concentrate after they've finished shopping for shoes. And much like shoes, the allure of a handbag is more about the immediate attraction than the durability, practicality or function. A man might own one battered up brown or black leather tri-fold wallet, a brief case and a back pack. This is not the case with most women. Purses, much like shoes, are purchased on a "must have it" rather than on a "really need it" basis. They come in various shapes, sizes, colors, textures and finishes. Some clutches are barely large enough to hold a lipstick and a credit card while others could give a woman sore shoulders due to the sheer weight of the bag when fully packed.

Grandmothers' bags can be the best purses of all. To a small child, the contents of those magical sacks could be treasure trove and seem never ending rather like the tapestry bag carried by Mary Poppins. Many of us can recall rummaging through the myriad compartments and slots within our grandmother's handbag during Sunday morning worship service. We'd discover life savers, chewing gum, small packets of Kleenex, embroidered hankies, a collapsible drinking cup, her pill box, scraps of paper, old receipts, and sometimes even a brightly colored, folding fan hiding deep within the recesses of her handbag.

The contents of a purse are a very intimate and private thing. Financial advisors have said that a great deal can be learned about a person by examining their money habits and going through their check book register. That checkbook register or debit card inventory can tell an advisor where a person likes to shop and how much money they spend on such things as food, clothing and entertainment. It can also point out particular habits or patterns such as going to the mall on Mondays or out to dinner on Friday nights and to the movies on Saturday afternoon. The Bible says that our treasury indicates the true desires of our heart and points out our priorities (Mathew 6:21). A person will only spend money on what is important to them or on what they desire to have or to keep.

Asking someone to discuss attitudes and habits surrounding their money is perceived to be invasive or a highly personal conversation. People can get downright touchy when their spending is called into question. That's perhaps why so many marriage counselors strongly advise that a couple sit down and seriously discuss their saving and spending habits as well as their willingness to live within a budget before walking down the aisle. Many marriage partners who would never even consider sexual infidelity will be found guilty of a financial indiscretion and of monetary secret keeping.

As ambassadors of God's kingdom we will need to be certain that we are aware of the power of our purse. If held in a pair of open palms, our purse can be used to unlock doors, feed the hungry, empower the powerless, heal those in need of healing, and enlarge the kingdom of God (Luke 4:18). A gift of money given with a grateful heart can be an act of worship unto the Lord. We also have a promise from the Lord that when we give freely and openly, he lavishes right back to us in the same measure (Luke 6:38). In this reciprocal relationship we become streams of providence and channels of blessing in the lives of others around us. God loves a cheerful giver and he loves to give good gifts to His children (2 Corinthians 9:7, Matthew 7:11).

If held in too tightly clinched fists, our purse can become a bottomless pit of want, disillusionment, despair, emptiness and compulsive behavior. Having money or accumulating possessions will not produce contentment; but the desire for money can produce the sins of envy, greed and dissatisfaction with what the Lord provides (Matthew 6:25, 34, Hebrews 13:10, James 3:16, 1 Timothy 6:10). Our purse can quickly become our prison and its strings the manacles that bind us if we forget that it is God who is the origin from whom every good and perfect thing comes (James 1:17). He can just as easily take away as he can give if we act foolishly with what he provides. In Leviticus chapter twenty five (25) the children of Israel were admonished to be good stewards of what God provided them and to always be thankful. These are wise words for fearfully wonderful women to follow.

If our eternal home is in heaven then we need to lay up treasures of eternal value rather than put all our trust and security in treasures that can be stolen, lost or destroyed (Matthew 6:19). To be rich in God is to be rich in deed (Luke 12:21). There is no sin in our owning nice things or accumulating wealth as long as those things or that wealth do not own us in return (Luke 12:14). True contentment is only found when we recognize our own sinfulness in light of God's unconditional love and goodness (1 John 4:10).That is because it is when we truly understand the gravity of our sin set against the majesty of Holy God's redemption that we can thank God that he does not treat us as we deserve. Recognizing that Jehovah -Jireh promises to provide all that we need and to give us the desires of our hearts if we will trust Him should make it easy for us to joyfully share all that we have with those around us. Such assurance should also provide the peace and stability that we need in an often fickle, ever shifting world of financial dishonesty, misappropriation and insecurity. (Philippians 4:6 -19, Psalm 37:4). As ambassadors, we have inherited stock in a heavenly and eternal kingdom with an endless portfolio and a bottomless treasure trove. We share an inheritance that has no end and have a heavenly Father who loves us unconditionally and promises to meet all our needs. From this supply. There is no greater security possible.

✳ ROADSIDE REFLECTIONS:

- Is there some "junk" jewelry or costume treasure that you need to remove from your treasure chest in exchange for the immeasurably valuable treasures that God longs to give? How do we begin the process of letting go of the earthly things that we value so that Christ can increase our stock shares within his heavenly kingdom?

- Are you a channel of blessing in the lives of others or do you hold on to worldly possessions or money too tightly?

ACCESSORIES THAT ENDURE A LIFETIME

Our accessory wrap is getting pretty well organized. We've collected our pearls and synchronized our watches. We've assembled individual pieces as well as paid attention to the smaller details that are all a part of our personal statement whether at work or at leisure. We've also selected a large enough purse to carry those items we will need close at hand while traveling with the Lord but have been careful that it isn't so large that it weighs us down. After all, it would be counterproductive to lighten our suitcases only to over stuff our handbags.

Before we set our accessory wrap aside and begin determining our cosmetic and beauty needs let's take a look at what are sure to be the always fashionable accessories that every fearfully, wonderful woman will want to include in her personal fashion statement. In the interest of following our goal of conserving space and reducing weight, this list includes only those items guaranteed to go with everything in an ambassador's wardrobe and to last an eternity.

What accessories should all the fashion forward, well dressed and fearfully wonderful women of God be wearing in and out of every season of life? An item by item description can be found in Proverbs chapter thirty-one.

- *Lips full of Praise*- Psalm 147:1

  o *Everybody likes the look of a fuller lip.*

- **Virtue**- Proverbs 31:10.

  o *This one tops the list because word has it that its value is far above rubies.*

- **Industrious hands**- Proverbs 31:13

- **A Fugal business mind**- Proverbs 31:16

- **A Charitable attitude**- Proverbs 31:20

- **Preparation and advance planning**- Proverbs 31: 21

- **Respect**- Proverbs 31:23

  o *It seems Aretha Franklin had it right. Respect is of utmost importance.*

- **Joyful heart**- Proverbs 31:25

- **Strength and honor**- Proverbs 31:25

- **The Fear of the Lord**- Proverbs 31:30

CHAPTER 9

The Cosmetics Case

I n reading the creation account found in Genesis chapter 1 beginning at verse two we see that God gave the earth form and light and beauty (Genesis 1:2). Each of these three elements is important aspects for all of God's creation. One can just imagine the great pride and artistic discipline God used as in verse eleven He brought forth grass and herbs, trees ripe with fruit and seeds for various plants, flowers and vegetation (Genesis 1:11). He thought of color, of light, of symmetry and of balance as in verse fourteen He established the changing of the seasons and in verse fifteen He flung the sun and the moon, the planets and every twinkling star up into the vast heavens (Genesis 1:14-15).

Has the work of any master artist ever compared to the beauty found in a crisp fall morning in the mountains of North Carolina? Can ink or oil placed on paper or canvas translate the exact shade and hue of the blue used by God to color the deepest depth of the ocean? Is there a crayon contained within the large box of sixty-four that could be used to duplicate that intricate and subtle shading of an individual rose, iris or lily that causes it to stand out among the rest? And tell me, does Solomon in all his magnificent regalia hold a candle to a single , frost covered daffodil pushing through the glistening snow on an early spring morning (Matthew 6:29)?

There is nothing wrong with desiring to be beautiful. God obviously considered these aesthetic qualities pleasing. Take a look at the butterflies, brightly colored birds, perfectly formed shells, and beautifully perfumed flowers that are his handiwork. Our God made things beautiful. Things of beauty bring Him pleasure in the same way that the beings created in his image, humans, enjoy things of beauty. Human beings have always recognized the value of beauty and perfection and have consequently responded by offering up the most beautiful or most perfect of their crafts, harvest, livestock, or fruit of their labor to God in acts of worship and adoration.

BEAUTY IS IN THE EYE OF ONE'S CULTURE

Acts of worship have also long included body modification and adornment. Throughout history and in almost every culture or religion, humans have altered their bodies to make them more appealing to their deities or to indicate which deity they worship, honor, or serve. These alterations range from the temporary to the permanent and from the minimal to the extreme. Whether we are discussing painting faces, piercing various body parts, tattooing the skin, elongating the neck, whittling the teeth or elaborately styling the hair; all human cultures contain forms of body modification which are directed by their individual cultural definitions of beauty or aesthetic preferences. While most cultures ascribe to gender specific cultural constructs of beauty, defining both the male and the female ideals of beauty, the longest list of rules and regulations or tightest restraints are usually found in cultural definitions of what is pleasing or acceptable in the appearance of the female.

If you've ever wondered how to get a glowing, streak- free, less orange self- tan, how to eliminate the first signs of gray hair, or how to get rid of those stubborn little laugh lines and extra five pounds; then you are responding to the standards of beauty contained within the culture of the United States of America. These constructs outline what our culture has deemed to be desirable, admirable, beautiful and valuable in the attributes of a human representative. Members of our society who do not conform to these beauty ideals will be picked last for kickball, left uninvited to the junior high dance, teased and taunted for their appearance, and possibly passed over for hiring, advancement or raises. Value judgments will be placed upon them if they are "too" fat, "too" tall, "too" short or "too" physically dismembered or impaired. This is because the culturally contained constructs of beauty set the standard to which all members of a society are compared. Members are evaluated, ranked, included and rewarded based upon how closely they come to the perfect ideal of that which is aesthetically desirable or pleasing. Within the United States we value youth, height, the appearance of health, and sensuality. Our cultural constructs of beauty display these values. Just take a quick stroll through a corner drugstore and count how many products promise a "healthy glow", a "youthful appearance" or increased sexual appeal.

The beauty products being offered today's women promise everything from looking five years younger to feeling five pounds thinner. Manufacturers assure their female consumers that using their product will enhance our looks, eliminate our odors, tighten our pores and leave us feeling kiss ably smooth and fresh as a summer day. A simple eight week trial of their product will reveal a noticeable improvement to the old and no longer valued us. We simply must have this product or that treatment because we can see clearer skin in moments, luxuriate in their foam, defy our age, look instantly younger and always be at our best. Their advertisements assure us that it is okay to spend hundreds of dollars for an intensively hydrating moisture treatment containing sea minerals and caviar…"because we're worth it".

CONFORMING TO THE STANDARDS

Being beautiful can be tricky business. One risk is that the standards of beauty are fickle and constantly changing. A woman may get implants to plump her breasts in the hopes of being found sensual one season only to learn that the braless look and sheer blouses are all the rage the next season. Short hair may be the fashion forward trend of one season only to be quickly followed by a mandate for long, luscious waves of hair that cascades down a woman's back. Twiggy thin and heroin chic replaces the full figured, more voluptuous shapes of Marilyn Monroe and Jane Russell, and the "natural look" cycles in and out with pink hair and shocking blue eye shadow.

Another risk in seeking to conform to standards of beauty is that these preferences can be regional or confined to a particular ethnic group or subculture. A woman could be a true work of beauty until she crosses the Mississippi divide or, for that matter, more than one state line. Then, suddenly it happens: a beauty blunder! Constantly seeking to be in style or to keep pace can be exhausting work because it is difficult to ascertain which standards are **the** standards. Simply taking a cross country airplane trip can be an exercise in frustration for the woman who has the need to fit in. She may discover that big hair is desired in Dallas while mall hair and bump- its were seen sported in Jersey and a more controlled coif is the sign of status on Rodeo Drive in Palm Beach, Florida. A fashion forward woman's only hope for conformity in this situation would seem to be to invest in wigs.

In the midst of these changes one thing remains constant: consumers will continue to crave the newest, latest, greatest and most improved formulas that the market has to offer all in an effort to keep up with this fast paced world by looking like we belong. Beauty has become something that we 'do' rather than something that we are. Perfection can be purchased and with the right cosmetic treatment the seasons of life can be reversed if not avoided altogether.

PRETTINESS, PAINT, PETTINESS AND SIN

As ambassadors of God's kingdom, is there anything wrong with sprucing up what God gave us? What about coloring our hair or injecting collagen into our lips? Is it a sin to paint our faces or to lift our sagging body parts? Can Christian women whittle away their waddle ? In order to answer these questions we must honestly determine our motivation for doing what we are doing. What is driving our desire to wear makeup, buy a padded bra, color our hair, or invest in liposuction, Botox and silicone? Obviously, if our beauty behavior can be tied to some unconfessed sinful desire, then we need to repent from that behavior. But we cannot and must not assume that women dress up, wear perfume, color their hair and paint their nails out of some sinful motivation. There are multiple motivations for being fashion forward and seeking to be beautiful. Some of these motives are healthy while others need to examined and replaced.

When we "put on our faces" are we seeking to enhance the fabulous features with which our creator endowed us, or, do we secretly wish that He had made us differently? Are we seeking to display the wonder of God's artistry, or, are we trying to hide what we perceive as a flaw or as an error on His part? If we do not like how we are shaped, formed and fashioned together by our maker then how can we be happy with Him? It would be difficult to praise a creator whom we feel has left us wanton or disappointed. If we do not love ourselves then how can we trust the love of the one who created us? Perhaps rather than cover up or surgically repair the thing that is offensive to us we need to evaluate why we are offended. Is it jealousy? Self- pity? Pride? Vanity? All of these motivations are sinful. Rather than considering ourselves an ugly duckling or feeling as if our facial features are something that we need to hide; we can cry out to our creator just as the psalmist cried out in the one hundred and nineteenth psalm asking God to reveal his purpose for making us as He did:

"Your hands made me and formed me; give me understanding to learn your commands... May your unfailing love be my comfort, according to your promise to your servant... Let your compassion come to me that I may live, for your law is my delight."- Psalm 119:73, 76-77

If our conformity to the fickle beauty standards established by our culture is the foundation for our validation and sense of self-worth then we are in serious trouble indeed. Besides seeking to build the foundation of our very being on shifting sands as previously discussed (see Matthew 7:24-27), from a practical perspective it is never a good idea to keep our self -esteem in a make-up bottle. Foundation and powder wash off and the admiration of people is fickle and fleeting. When the crowds have gone home and we come to the end of our day we will have to face our true self in the bathroom mirror. We can't live our lives behind a mask forever. Eventually, we all must scrub our faces and come clean with who we really are. Therefore, it is best to find our validation and worth in something non-wavering, steadfast and eternal. Every fearfully wonderful woman will have good hair days, bad hair days, fat days and days of feeling fabulous but those temporal conditions should not determine her true sense of self (Philippians 4:4-9). Definitions of beauty are subjective and relative. The unconditional love and goodness of God provide a much more stable and enduring bedrock upon which to place our trust (Psalm 91:1-16). A low self-esteem can be best remedied by learning who we are in Christ and not by visiting with the sales woman behind the department store cosmetics counter. Truthfully, most of us usually feel worse about ourselves after the woman in the black lab coat behind the cosmetics counter informs us of all our flaws and imperfections. We are embarrassed to have presented ourselves in public in such disarray and purchase her offerings in the hopes of looking better the next time.

We need to ask ourselves what messages our body modifications and cosmetic alterations send to others regarding the deities we may serve, the values that we follow, or the gods to whom we pledge our reverence. To whose standard are we conforming anyway (Romans 12:1-2)? The prince of this earthly realm is a direct enemy to the God who sits on the throne above all things. That's why it is always a good idea to find out the origins and meanings of a particular body modification before submitting our bodies to them. Tattooing a playboy bunny, a swastika , an ankh, or some other symbol that might have a meaning which would dishonor the Lord or call our values and morals into question is not advisable for an ambassador of God's kingdom. Before submitting to a body modification with questionable symbolism or interpretation, an ambassador of Christ should do her research, seek out the opinions and views of others whom she honors, and seek the counsel of her God. This is particularly true when considering tattoos, brandings, and some ritualistic piercings. Many of the faddish tribal and Eastern symbols available as fashion statements in today's popular culture find their origins in worship to pagan gods or have meanings drawn from religions or philosophies that oppose Christian views. While the wearer of the symbol may think that she is sending one message, the interpreter of the symbol may read an entirely different and opposing one. We can't always avoid others passing judgment unaware or misunderstanding the purpose of our appearance but we should do everything within our power to put our best foot forward and to represent our Father well. If our bodies are the temples of the living God then we certainly do not want to mark them with a symbol that may be read as "Holiday Inn" or "Welcome Home" by some demon or ungodly minion.

✖ ROADSIDE REFLECTIONS:

- We have been discussing the very serious issue of women literally killing themselves or at least engaging in very risky practices all in an effort to achieve cultural standards of beauty. While scripture does not speak specifically about cosmetic enhancements of any kind we do know that coveting what we do not have is sin and that lying is a practice of the old self. We are called to be renewed in knowledge in the image of our creator (Colossians 3:10).

- How then do we begin to balance out *becoming* all that God desires us to be with *being* in the world and desiring to be beautiful without *begrudging* those who may be younger, sexier or more physically beautiful than we?

- How do we know when we've crossed the line or gone too far in our quest for beauty?

LEGALISM AND THE LADY

While scripture offers no direct instruction prohibiting wearing cosmetics, coloring one's hair or piercing one's ears, it does give us some guiding principles that we should use to make such decisions. For example, scripture does tell us that we have a loving Heavenly Father who is concerned about anything that concerns us (Philippians 4:6, 1 Peter 5:7). Our desire to dress in a manner that pleases Him is something about which we can and should consult Him.

Every fearfully wonderful woman should begin her decision process by consulting the Holy Spirit who abides within her and then discern whether she has a personal conviction regarding a manner of dress or adornment (John 16:8). If a particular dress feels too short or too tight or if her makeup seems too heavy it could be that she has a conviction regarding those things. Of course, many of these decisions can be determined based upon her age, body structure and occupation or present activity, but feeling uncomfortable could be a gentle nudging offered by the Holy Spirit to indicate that something is inappropriate for us . We must be sensitive to these gentle nudges. We must also be careful that we do not assume that everyone has the same convictions (Romans 14:1-5). What might be perfectly acceptable for another sister in this band of travelers may not be permissible for you. Ask the Holy Spirit to put a check in you or to reveal to you anything that is out of character for your walk, for your calling, or for your testimony. The Holy Spirit provides all ambassadors with the wisdom and discernment needed to make decisions that honor and please the Lord (Proverbs 3:13-15). Remember, our standard is Christ Jesus, not Cover Girl or Maybelline, and not each other. Having said that, it is always wise to consult another fearfully wonderful and fabulous woman of God if we aren't quite sure about a particular look. She will be able to honestly tell us how other people will discern and judge our attempt at being fashionable.

Scripture offers clear instruction against being vain or silly (Ecclesiastes 11:10, Isaiah 59:4, Romans 8:20, Philippians 2:3-4)). It is quite feasible that a fearfully wonderfully woman who has developed too great a focus on appearance is shifting her focus away from things of greater importance to the kingdom of God. Spending precious time, emotion, or finances on something as fleeting as our appearance is not being a wise steward of God (Luke 16:10-12). Being consumed with the perceived flaws of our appearance might prevent us from finding contentment and learning to be satisfied with God's provision (Proverbs 31:30). As fearfully wonderful women, we need to examine how much of our money , time and energy is being spent in front of the mirror, at the cosmetics counter, or in discussing or seeking assurance from others regarding our appearance. If things seem out of balance we need to be honest with the Lord and with ourselves and then try to determine the root cause for our drawer full of lipsticks, outrageous Sephora bill, or over-processed, bleached out roots. Our compulsion, if left unchecked, can spiral into an identifiable addiction if we are not cautious.

Cosmetic enhancements and surgical procedures much like tattoos or potato chips can be psychologically addictive and often one procedure leads to countless more. The American Society for Aesthetic Plastic Surgery estimates that over ten million Americans subjected themselves to one form of surgical cosmetic correction or another in the year 2008 alone. According to their research, ninety- two percent (92%) of those patients were women. Some of the most dramatic increases in cosmetic surgical procedures have been among younger women and teenagers with some girls requesting breast augmentation from their parents as gifts for their sixteenth birthday. How sad it is to consider that so many young women are unhappy with the physical provision of their body that God has given them. Sadder still is the fact that they are willing to endure painful cosmetic procedures along with their health and possibly even their life in an effort to achieve a more pleasing appearance.

As ambassadors a better focus and use of our time would be to work on making our spiritual being and our hearts as beautiful as possible. God created us as spirits who are housed within physical tents. These temporary lodgings of flesh and bone will eventually decay (2 Corinthians 5:1-10). It is inevitable. They are designed that way. No cosmetic procedure or anti- aging formula is going to stop death from arriving on time and at your door just as God scheduled (Psalm 39:5, Psalm 144:4). Most cosmetic procedures eventually require touch- ups; breast implants require replacement and liposuctioned fat sooner or later finds its way back home. While we all desire to be healthy and attractive for all the days that we live on this planet, we need to also be realistic. Gravity happens. Skin ages. Bodies decay. Our eternal spirit should be our focus as that is what God sees, judges and created to be forever with Him (Matthew 23:28, 1 Samuel 16:7).

DISCOVERING THE BEAUTY BALANCE

In our desire for sanctification and holiness we also want to be certain that the pendulum does not swing in the opposite direction. Those around us appreciate it when we brush our teeth and wear deodorant just as much as other dinner guests appreciated the Biblical custom of foot washing before sitting down to dine with travelers who had walked a great distance. Our natural body chemistry and bodily functions do produce odors. These can be offensive to others. Ambassadors representing the kingdom of God need to be certain that the breath we are sharing is not so offensive that it prevents others from hearing the good news that we bring. While we might not be able to totally justify the expense of that color-lock lip gloss, chip resistant nail polish or ergonomically designed blush brush; we can certainly consider the purchase of a bar of soap, a good toothbrush, a comb, and breath cleansing fluoride gel allowable business expenditures. Remember, we are in this world for a purpose. We are ambassadors and representatives of God's kingdom. Our appearance is a direct reflection upon Him and of Him to others. What message does an unkempt, disheveled and foul smelling ambassador send about her King, her values and her fellow kingdom members? Everything we do, including how we care for this body that the Lord has entrusted to us, should be done to the glory of God and to the benefit of His kingdom (1 Corinthians 10:31). The heavens declare the glory of God and so should we (Psalm 19). We must remember as ambassadors of God's kingdom that we have been bought by Christ's blood sacrifice and now have an obligation to glorify our Lord and Savior in our physical bodies (1 Corinthians 6:20). We must ascribe the glory due God's holy name (Psalm 29:1-2).

We must also remember that when we were bought with the blood of Jesus we were set free to worship and to follow him. We are his disciples. We hear his voice and we follow his leading (John 10:27).We are the sheep of his pasture and the people of his kingdom (Psalm 100:1-3). God designed us for his good pleasure and for His purpose. We must not be the blind sheep of a religious doctrine or a dogmatic set of legalisms or laws. Christ set us free from such restraints and gave us the Holy Spirit to instruct us and to guide us. As his followers, we must be careful not to become entangled again in a list of rules and restraints constructed by human beings and dictated by religious ritual. Where the spirit of the Lord is there is liberty (Galatians 5:1-6).

While we must not use the grace that God has given us as an excuse to live a life of sin or to be an offense to others; we do not want to cheapen its value by conforming to rules and regulations that he has not given us. No woman can serve two masters (Matthew 6:24). The letter of the law kills the human spirit by bringing it under condemnation and oppression (2 Corinthians 3:6-8). Systems of governance based upon strict rules and over bearing accountability often lead to human rebellion or feelings of inadequacy and hopelessness. This is because no one can measure up to constant scrutiny or live a life that is free from error. It is by grace that we have been redeemed and it is under that grace that we must operate in self-discipline and discernment (1 Peter 1:13-19). If a fearfully wonderful woman of God wishes to wear three-quarter length sleeves and not to cut her hair then she is free in the Lord to follow those desires. If another fabulous female follower of Christ does not share those convictions then she must operate under the discernment given her by her Lord and Master. Each woman has a Heavenly Father who sees her and who judges her life and her deeds (1 Peter 1:17). Each will be held accountable to the standard that he alone can prescribe. Every Fearfully wonderful woman of God has a responsibility to carefully listen to the leading of the Lord, to search out the scriptures and then to trust her own discernment when determining what manner of dress is correct for her. Seeking to live up to the standard that God has established in his Word and to actively manifest the fruit of the spirit in our lives should be every ambassador's primary objective (Galatians 5:22-23).

Imagine trying to perform an intricate and complicated surgical procedure on a patient's heart valves with only one sighted eye. How many of us would trust the outcome of our loved one's surgery to the attention of such a physician? More than one of our Christian sister's hearts are severely damaged because of others who seek to correct the minor fault that they may see within her while a large two by four is protruding from their own eye (Matthew 7:3). Let us focus on our own faces and inspect our own clothing and trust our sister's appearance to the Lord's care.

BURNING ON WITHOUT BURNING OUT

Ever notice while watching an" age defying" make over on an afternoon television show one of the first things they do is color the overly excited volunteering woman's graying hair (right after they cut it all off) ? Within our youth oriented culture, growing old is portrayed as something for women to fear and the appearance of white or graying hair is supposedly the first tale-tell sign of the downward spiral towards that dreaded occurrence.

It seems as if aging baby boomers will do anything to avoid looking their real age. Forget about aging gracefully too. Today's aging generation is convinced that in order to compete or to stay of value and relevant they need to defy age altogether. Our economy is filled with potions, lotions and hair products purported to turn back the hands of time and to restore our youth. Defying aging as if it were a curse has become a new national obsession.

Every "woman of a certain age" desires to be beautiful. Every human being wants to be deemed useful or of value to their society. Having a healthy body image is often over simplified to being happy with one's body shape, weight and size. A healthy body attitude also involves how a woman accepts her age and the changes that occur while moving through the various phases of life. Be advised that each of these phases within a woman's life is guaranteed to make changes in three basic areas: hips, hormones and hair.

The process of being at peace with our body is a spiritual one and comes from recognizing the foundational truths which we have already discussed. These truths hold more validity than what any beauty editor or fashion magazine may try to tell us and remain true whether a woman is twenty-one, fifty-four (the author's present age), or well beyond. Biblical truths have the power to set us free from the trap of feeling that we are no longer beautiful or viable simply because we have passed a certain age marker or have begun to sprout a head full of glorious, glistening gray hair. Knowing some simple truths about who we are and how God sees us can cast growing older in a totally different light and free us from cultural dictates regarding what is proper beauty for an older woman. Consider these simple statements contained in God's Word:

"Gray hair is a crown of splendor; it is attained by a righteous life." – Proverbs 16:31

"The glory of young men is their strength, gray hair the splendor of the old."- Proverbs 20:29

These Scriptures tell us that having gray hair is the outward sign of a righteous life and is viewed by God as a crown. Luke 12:7 suggests that God took great pains in his design right down to numbering the hairs on our heads. An artist only spends that much time in the creation of something that he loves or values dearly. It is the object of focus in an artwork that gets the greatest amount of attention. It would be logical to conclude that if God took time to number the hairs on our heads then he also gave consideration to the color and texture. Perhaps if the cultural standards of beauty described gray hair as being splendid rather than drab, and as a crown rather than as a sign of lost youth and faded beauty; fewer women would want to wash it right out of their heads. If white hair were deemed as a reward for righteous living wouldn't we want to flaunt it rather than pluck it, color it or try some other ingenious way to conceal its presence on our head? What beauty pageant winner or home coming queen ever tried to hide her tiara or crown?

When we were twelve we couldn't wait to be older and accounted for every segment of our age. We would proudly announce that we we're " twelve and three quarters" rather than merely twelve. Suddenly, when a woman reaches twenty-nine (29) she is expected to be coy by keeping her true age a secret. Our culture is full of cheeky phrases such as: "Twenty-nine and holding" or " Thirty-five again". What changed? Aren't we that same proud little girl only with an older body? What happened to her spirit and her spunk? When did "old" become a dirty word in our culture? When did getting older , which is a natural process, become something to defy or to fight? Growing older does not have to be associated with being ill or disabled or no longer of value. Aging is a process not a disease, and each of us will go through that process. It is God's plan.

As fearfully wonderful women we should be praising God for giving us each day on this earth. Rather than seeking to defy our age shouldn't the cry of our hearts be like that of the psalmist who prayed: "Teach us to number our days aright, that we may gain a heart of wisdom" (Psalm 90:12)? We might pattern our life goals after 1 Corinthians 1:8 and place our life in the Lord's hands asking that He keep us strong and present us blameless before God's throne. After all, it is God who numbers our days (Psalm 39:4-6, Psalm 139:16). Living for Him and following His plan for our life is actually a very intelligent life plan. What we as godly women do when we are younger- whether it be physically, emotionally, psychologically or spiritually- will be reaped by us when we are older (Galatians 6:7). We should plan ahead and sow plentifully while we are younger. God promises to add purposeful and pleasant days to those people who follow his precepts (Deuteronomy 5:33, Proverbs 3:1,Proverbs 9:11). Sowing richly into the lives of younger women while we have the opportunity will yield a bountiful harvest of blessing when we are older (Proverbs 31:28, 2 Corinthians 9:6).

Perhaps some of us have discovered that our "golden" years are really "silver" and that silver requires polishing, housing correctly and special care to avoid becoming tarnished, pitted and of diminished value. If we are going to be treasured vessels for the Lord's service, then the question remains regarding what sort of care we will take as we go through the aging process. As older women within the Body of Christ, will we be grumpy, tarnished and gray or glistening, godly and gloriously glowing? What will our conversation and our actions model to those fearfully wonderful females who walk behind us on this journey of life? After having counseled many young women about being "fearfully and wonderfully made" will we practice what we preach? When the first wrinkles appear and the creeks and cracks of the morning wake up begin to be accompanied by increased aches and pains will we still declare that our creator fashioned us with wisdom and reverence? Will we huff and puff about the extra bulges and sags or continue to sing praise to our creator's name? Will we submit to the surgeon's knife or yield to God's wisdom? What testimony will the declarations made while in the midst of menopausal hot flashes, night sweats and insomnia speak to those young women who look up to us or who choose to emulate us? Will we still be in awe of God's handiwork (Psalm 139: 14). God forbid that our negativity and self- talk about aging and slowing down undo our counsel to our daughters and our grand-daughters. May we determine now to seek to glorify God and to reflect His image all the days of our lives. May we ever be gracious and glorious glowing embers to the glory of God.

Hopefully our aging will provide us the wisdom needed to encourage other women to take better care of themselves in every facet of their lives; to love themselves and to nourish their physical, emotional, mental and spiritual well- being. Perhaps our pearls of adornment can serve as memory stones to help us in counseling younger women to avoid the same mistakes we made by neglecting ourselves or by putting our spiritual and emotional needs behind the daily rush and the immediate needs of our children or our household. We want to counsel these beautiful glowing embers of God's grace and exhibits of His awesome handiwork to burn on rather than to burn out. Water cannot be drawn from an empty well and a drained and exhausted woman cannot provide nurturing support to her children, her husband or for those to whom she has been called to minister.

In Exodus 3: 1-15, Moses accepts his destiny and meets his God in the presence of a burning bush. The voice of almighty God calling from within that glowing bush told Moses, who was currently tending his father in laws' sheep out in the desert heat, that He had big plans for him (Exodus 3:1-2). Moses was going to be the promised deliverer for the Children of Israel who were now being held in bondage within Egypt.

Something about this scrub brush burning in the desert obviously got Moses' attention; otherwise He would not have walked over to take a closer look. The bush in this story wasn't anything extraordinary in and of itself. It was a very ordinary type of scrub that grew in the desert where Moses was tending flocks. Sudden combustion or a brush fire would not have been an uncommon sight either given the combination of the abundance of dry thicket and the intense direct rays of the desert sun. Moses wasn't attracted to the bush. He was attracted to the fire. He recognized that the fire contained within that little bush was anything but mundane and that it could not have been caused by spontaneous combustion or desert heat. Moses was amazed that this simple desert scrub that stood blazing in the heat was not being overcome or consumed by the indigo blue flames emanating from its very core (Exodus 3:3). That little bush was ignited by the indwelling presence of God. Almighty God was at the core of that little desert plant and as she surrendered to His presence He burned brightly within her and yet did not consume her by his demands. He set her ablaze but never used her up.

Ladies, as we become silver headed ambassadors for God may we be as that burning bush for those younger women who look up to us. May the fire of His presence that burns within our hearts never burn out. May we glow and glisten whether our hair be flaxen, golden, silver or gray. May we reflect our Father's beauty and be set ablaze by His presence in our lives . May we never grow weary because we have learned to draw deeply from the source of living water (John 4:10). After having drawn from His wells, may we become overflowing springs of blessing rather than old broken down cisterns in the lives of others (John 7:38, Jeremiah 2:13). We will not need to find our beauty in a mask of make-up or in a bottle of hair color if our faces radiate and glow because we have spent time in the presence of God Almighty (Exodus 34:35). Our beauty will come from the someone that we are rather than from the something that we wear.

ABSOLUTE THREE IN ONE OIL

In Jeremiah Chapter eight (8) the prophet is considering the maladies and sin sick condition of the people of God and asks why their daughters should be found in such a pitiful state when there is a balm in Gilead readily available to them that can heal and restore (Jeremiah 8:22). That balm is still available to us today. It is the fabulous and original "three in one" oil because this oil originates from the holy three in one; that is the Father, the Son and the Holy Spirit, and it is the remedy for all that ails each of us as well as for our sin sick society at large. This priceless oil is guaranteed to work efficiently and effectively in all situations and on most maladies. It heals what is bleeding and sore. It restores that which is broken or shattered. This soothing oil brings comfort to that which is painful and hurting and provides refreshment and strength to the weary and worn; and best of all, it is absolutely free and in abundant supply for all God's fearfully wonderful women. It is also the absolute ultimate beauty product and regardless of our age or phase of life this one product should be included in each of our daily beauty regimes.

The fabulous beauty product of which I speak is the anointing oil of the Holy Spirit. In Psalm 23:5-6 we read that Our Lord anoints our heads with oil and that our cups run over with the abundance of that anointing. In biblical history it was only someone who was of importance, worth or potential that was recognized in such a manner. This type of anointing can be equated with being knighted or commissioned. Recall that biblical kings such as David and Saul were anointed at the point of their coronation (1 Samuel 9, 16:1-13). Being anointed by the Lord means that we have been chosen and that each of us is someone very special to him. It should bring a smile to our faces and put a twinkle in our eyes to realize that we are loved, called, chosen, ordained and of inordinate value to him. Our Lord has given us the oil of gladness (Psalm 54:7, Isaiah 61).We should glow with joy and be energized from within at the thought of such love and value. And because our cups run over with this oil we have no reason to be stingy or to practice restraint with our use of it. We can lavish this precious oil on ourselves and on all those around us who are hurting or sick. We can pack it in our purses and apply it freely as a healing balm, a refreshing tonic and a comforting salve on ourselves as well as on all those who cross our path. Our provision will not run out. Our cup will not run dry. Our Lord will multiply our supply as we freely pour out this precious "three in one" oil on others (1 Kings 4:1-7).

CHAPTER 10

Our Foot Locker

Foot lockers were originally named as such because of their location at the foot of the beds of Army soldiers. These individually assigned trunks are used to store battle gear and personal belongings within the barracks or bunk houses of military troops. Every branch of military service has the equivalent of a foot locker which is usually left behind at the home base during a deployment or move out due to its larger size and weight. When going out on a mission, it's important for the solider on assignment to pack enough personal supplies to support them for however long they are going to be in the field, and since a soldier is helpless if unarmed it's crucial to both pack and to protect one's weapons at all costs. Smaller, more transportable bags such as packs, duffle bags, flight bags, and load out cases, day bags, sea bags and duty packs are used by the deployed military member. These bags in essence are the tool bags or smaller equipment lockers used to hold all items necessary for engaging in the anticipated battle or conflict while away from the home base.

OUR BATTLE ASSIGNMENT

As ambassadors of God's heavenly kingdom we are automatically enlisted in his army. The very moment that we accepted Christ as our Lord and dedicated our lives to his service battle lines were drawn and an enemy assignment was sent out against us. As Christians, the difficulties and trials that we're going through are much more than a mere " human struggles". We are engaged in warfare against the enemies of powers and principalities, strongholds, arguments and false pretenses (Ephesians 6:12). Anything that is not obedient to the rule of God must be brought captive and submitted to his authority. 2 Corinthians 10:3-5 reminds us:

"For though we live in the world, we do not wage war as the world does. The weapons we fight with are not the weapons of the world. On the contrary, they have divine power to demolish strongholds. We demolish arguments and every pretension that sets itself up against the knowledge of God, and we take captive every thought to make it obedient to Christ."

The good news is that as Children of God and members of His heavenly kingdom we already know the outcome of this battle and we are on the winning side (Revelation 21:15-27). Our enemy, Satan, is a defeated foe (Ephesians 1:19-23, Revelation 20:10). He is no match for God Almighty and Jesus has already secured the victory for us (1 Corinthians 15:24-28,15:57, 1 John 3:8). We do not need to fear our enemy or his minions as Christ has given us authority over him and the Holy Spirit living in us is far more powerful and more wise than Satan can ever imagine (Luke 10:19, 2 Corinthians 10:4,Colossians 2:15 1 John 4:4). Our Commander in Chief commands victory for us as our king (Psalm 44:4).

We must remember that Satan is a liar and that he works through deception and falsehood. The truth of Jesus has set us free and exposed his trickery (Luke 21:8, John 8:32). Our enemy has no power or foothold in the lives of God's children unless we willfully surrender territory to him through our sin and deliberate disobedience (Romans 8:2, Galatians 5:1). If we draw near to our Father and resist the devil he will flee from us (James 4:7-10). We can fix our eyes on Jehovah Nissi, our banner, and follow our shepherd into the valley of the shadow of death knowing that no weapon formed against us shall prosper and that if God is with us we have nothing to fear (Exodus 16:10, Isaiah 54:17, Romans 8:28-31).

Fearfully wonderful women rest assured in God's unfailing love and know that anything and everything that touches our lives has been either allowed by our Father or directly orchestrated by Him. He will not give us any burden that is too heavy or task that is too difficult (1 Corinthians 10:13). He has thoroughly equipped us and prepared us for the hand battle in which we are now embroiled. He is the God of the present circumstance and He can use it for his glory and His honor as well as for our best. (Genesis 50:20, 1 Kings 12:24).

Though Satan is already defeated, he is still seeking to stop God's kingdom and rule from being established here on earth by inciting people to rebel and enticing them to sin (1 Chronicles 21:1). Our enemy seeks to cripple and to destroy as many of God's children as possible (John 10:10). Some of his favorite tactics are to sow discord or disunity, to spread lies or to bring false accusations and to confuse or confound God's children with doubt and fear (Zechariah 3:1-2, John 8:44, 1 Corinthians 14:33, Revelation 12:10). He also uses unwitting human beings to do his bidding and to inflict pain and suffering on others (Job 1:6-19). Our enemy's ultimate desire is to prevent as many people from hearing and accepting the good news of Jesus and of salvation as he possibly can. If he is going down, which he knows he is, then he desires to take as many captives with him as he is able (Matthew 25:41).

Being in a battle or living in a war zone is probably not an image that many of us choose to conjure up or a lifestyle that we would choose to embrace; but the Bible is very clear in explaining that all of us are engaged in this spiritual battle. Choosing to ignore those facts will not make the battle go away. We cannot live as an ostrich with our head buried underground. Our enemy is real and He knows who we are. He knows our weaknesses and our vulnerabilities. He has studied our routines and our habits. He has assigned his foot soldiers and spies to report our comings and goings. Our enemy never sleeps or retreats. He is always on the prowl seeking those whom he can maim or destroy. He is serious about this battle and we should be just as serious if we do not wish to be a casualty of war

It is important to note here, that unlike soldiers fighting in human scrimmages and assigned to particular battle operations, soldiers of the Lord do not get to leave the battlegrounds or go home for rest and relaxation at the end of an assigned tour of duty. While it is true that the Lord does shadow us under His wing and does provide times of rest and recuperation; we are instructed to be ever vigilant and constantly prepared for combat (1 Peter 5:8).

If we are living as we should as members of God's army then the foot locker that is stationed at the foot of our home base bunking should be empty of our armor, weapons and other battle gear because we are always dressed, always armed and ever expecting an enemy encounter. The only time a soldier of the Lord would take off her armor would be when she is sheltered safely under the wing of the Almighty and securely protected within his hiding place (Psalm 91:1-2). It is there and there alone that she is safe from Satan's schemes and snares (Psalm 91:3). It is there that the Lord God Almighty becomes her refuge and her shield (Psalm 91:4). We can pour out our hearts to our Abba- Father and ask Him to rebuke the adversary who is pursuing us and to dismiss the enemy assignments sent out against us. All the infinite power and wisdom of the ultimate Godhead is on the side of his daughters who seek to do his will. The Lord will send out his strength to uphold us in the battle (Psalm 68:28). He will restore our souls and renew our vitality.

ROADSIDE REFLECTION:

- Does the concept of being in a spiritual battle frighten you or inspire you on? How skilled are you in identifying the enemy and his tactics? Do you approach daily life fully armored or are you a "Christian streaker" running through the battlefield naked?

Our Armor

Since all ambassadors of Christ are engaged in a battle and living on a battlefield it might be a good idea to familiarize ourselves with the weapons that our Commander in Chief has given us. Our Father has entrusted a very specific and uncommon set of armor and weapons to our care and use (2 Corinthians 10:4-5). These weapons are designed to meet our enemies whom Paul identified as not being of flesh and blood but as spiritual forces of evil and as rulers and authorities in the heavenly realms and the dark world (Ephesians 6:12). Paul also explained that these weapons function to pull down strongholds, to cast down arguments, and to destroy every proud and arrogant thing that seeks to stop the rule of God (2 Corinthians 10:3-5). This would include our own fleshly desires and attitudes and as well as any and all ambassadors of our enemy's kingdom.

Dressing out in armor to engage in spiritual warfare may seem silly to Christians within today's modern culture. Armor and weapons are not a common part of our daily routines. However, the followers of Christ living during the time in which Paul wrote the book of Ephesians understood what it meant to live under the rule of a foreign army and to be an occupied nation. Fully dressed Roman soldiers , legions and battalions were common sightings within their communities and on their streets. It was from this imagery that Paul drew his illustration for the armor that every Christian needs to wear before going out to withstand and to defeat the endless onslaught of attacks being hurled against us by our enemy, Satan, and his demonic hosts. Choosing not to dress out in the armor which God provides us will not remove us from the battle. Such a decision will simply leave us defenseless and naked against the enemies' advances. Christian streakers are certain to take a beating on the spiritual battlefield and seldom survive for long.

In Ephesians Chapter six (6) Paul details the full set of armor that have been issued to every follower of Christ. He begins his instruction in Ephesians 6:10 by telling us to *"be strong in the Lord and in the power of His might"*. We must each immediately recognize that the battle is the Lord's and that none of us can defeat the enemy through our own cunning or human devises (Zechariah 4:6). We must stand on the promises given to us in God's Word and commit our situation to His plan and perfect will. Our faith allows us to proclaim that the promises of God are ours in this given moment and present circumstance (1 John 5:4-5, 2 Corinthians 1:20). We will prevail in faith and in prayer. We must also remember that God and Satan are not equals nor does Satan possess all the same attributes as those of God. Satan is a created being and God is his creator. Remember also that all the resources of God are available to us through our inheritance. Satan has no such assembly or power from which to draw. His resources and capabilities are limited while ours are infinite.

Paul tells us to put on the whole armor of God if we are going to be able to stand against the wiles of the devil (verse 11). Every fearfully wonderful woman of God has been provided a wardrobe of warfare. The obvious conclusion from Paul's writing is that we need to wear this armor at all times since we never know when our enemy will strike. We are also to wear each piece as each piece serves a distinct and separate function. Wearing the entire set of armor is important as Paul tells us again in Ephesians 6:13 to put on all of it and not to leave off any piece. We have already examined the battle shoes of our armor in Chapter seven (7) of this book. The other components of our battle gear, in order of appearance, include:

1. Belt of Truth – Ephesians 6:14

Satan is a liar and as such can only be defeated with truth. His tactics of planting doubt and confusion cannot stand up to the truth of God's word. Remember that Jesus proclaimed that He is truth and that it is the truth that sets us free (John 8:32, John 14:6). Satan speaks in half-truths and conjectures to cause doubt and speculation. He even misquotes scripture, which is why it is so vitally important for fearfully wonderful women to correctly hide scripture away in their hearts. Knowing scripture and the truth of God's promises will assure victory against Satan's lies and perversion of God's word (Psalm 119:11). Jesus combated Satan's attacks against him in the wilderness with scripture because He knew that our enemy could not argue or debate the absolute truth presented in God's word (Matthew 4:1-11). If God says it, then it is settled. There can be no debate. The truth of God is the belt that holds in our vital organs. It protects our inward being, our heart and our emotional responses or "gut feelings". It fastens us in securely at our very core.

2. The Breastplate of God's Righteousness – Ephesians 6:14

There is not a single woman past or present who has been made righteous based upon her own merit. It is only through the blood sacrifice of Jesus Christ we are righteous in the eyes of God (Romans 5:1). Our enemy will seek to condemn us and to cause us to believe that we are unworthy of God's favor and of his unconditional love. He is the accuser of the brethren (Revelation 12:7-12, Job 1). Knowing who we are in Christ and being fully assured that we are justified through our faith will help us to stand against Satan's condemnation (Romans 8:1, Ephesians 2:8-9, Hebrews 4:15-16). One of Satan's favorite attacks is on our security. He seeks to cause us to doubt God's love. The breastplate protects our hearts and reminds us that God's approval of us is unconditional and is grounded in the fact that He sent His Son to die for us. His grace and mercy are not predicated upon our personal merit. God looks at his daughter's through the grace covering of Jesus and sees us spotless and blameless as a result. His love is eternal, unconditional, freely available and greater than all our sin (1 John 4:16-18, Romans 8:38-39). Remember , our salvation and justification is not about who we are but rather about whose we are.

3. Shoes of the Gospel of Peace – Ephesians 6:15

We have already spent a great deal of time in Chapter seven (7) of this book examining our battle boots. These boots are made for walking out our inheritance, for taking claim of our territory, and for stomping out the works of our enemy. Paul is speaking in these verses in Ephesians chapter six (6) of the mighty steel toed, spike heeled boots similar to the ones worn by the Roman army. These battle boots will help us firmly take our stand and stomp on the head of our enemy.

But scripture also refers to these shoes as being the shoes of the gospel of peace. They are the sandals like those of Peter that we latch on our feet to follow our Lord wherever He leads; whether it be into prisons, hospitals, or directly into the heart of enemy territory (Luke 4:17-21). As good will ambassadors, we must always be ready to spread the good news of God's love and salvation through Jesus (Matthew 28:18-20, 1 Peter 3:15). Being prepared means having our shoes readily available or already latched on our feet.

These same sandals are the shoes that bring us boldly into the throne room of grace because these are the shoes given to the followers of the only gospel that established our peace with God and established our relationship with Him (Hebrews 4:14-16).

4. Shield of Faith – Ephesians 6:16

Paul states that the shield of faith is the piece of armor that quenches all the fiery darts of our enemy. Our faith is the shield that provides us protection against the insults, lies and burning accusations that the enemy hurls against us. The blistering sting of his bitter and vile spew is drowned and rendered powerless in the washing and renewing blood of Jesus Christ (Revelation 7:14). Our shield prevents that devious serpent's fangs from piercing our flesh and depositing their venomous poison of condemnation, self- loathing, doubt and despair. When we raise it high above our heads and carry it before us into battle it becomes an impenetrable barrier between Satan's attacks and our heads and hearts.

5. Helmet of Salvation – Ephesians 6:17

This piece of armor protects our minds from being infiltrated with thoughts that are contrary to the word or will of God. 1 Corinthians 10:15 reminds us that our battle is against thoughts, arguments and pretenses that rise up in disobedience to the truth of God's word. The major battleground for any Christian is being fought on the battlefield of the mind. We are to bring any thought that does not align with the word of God into obedience to the mind of Christ. Virtually anything that we are thinking that is not of God is of the flesh or the enemy (Mark 7:20-23). These thoughts must be brought captive and destroyed before they take root and begin to grow. It is when we dwell on a sinful or fleshly thought that it becomes an action and after that when it is fully developed it springs forth as sin (James 1:13-15).

Our helmet of salvation also allows us to know the mind of Christ and to operate in the wisdom and discernment of the Holy Spirit (Romans 8:23, 1 John 2:20). The helmet is placed upon the head or over the control center of the body. It is through this helmet that we allow the Holy Spirit to lead and to guide or to be our authority. When the Holy spirit is allowed to speak to us and to instruct us then we live and move completely connected to the fathomless depth of God's knowledge and directly in tune to his counsel (John 14:26, Acts 17:28). The full power of the Godhead is actualized within us and operates through us when we wear our helmet of salvation (John 7:28, Acts 1:8). It is then that we can rely upon the Holy Spirit to give us direction and instruction in the present situation and to make God's purpose and plan in it perfectly clear (2Corinthians 3:5). Our absolute surrender to God's authority and Lordship activates the indwelling power of the Holy Spirit and His full discernment and wisdom is made available to us.

6. Sword of the Spirit - Ephesians 6:17

It is at this point, in verse seventeen (17) of the passage, that Paul shifts from discussing our armor, or our defensive protections, to actually introducing an offensive weapon that we can use to attack and to destroy the works of our enemy. This weapon is the sword of the spirit, which Paul says in the word of God. When our enemy comes to tempt us with lies, doubts and sins we can rely upon the fact that God is with us, and then fight back and go forward on the attack using our sword. We can confidently tear down our enemy's strongholds and destroy his evil works. No matter how strong the presence of evil or how great the pressures of sin we know that we are in God and that he has already overcome our enemy (John 16:33, 1 John 4:4, Psalm 23:4).

We move forward in faith because we take God at His word and we take up His word to tear down the powers and principalities of our enemy. As His ambassadors, we can stand on His word as our sure foundation and use His word to silence and to rebuke our enemy. We can recite it to our souls and our minds, call it out to our Father, and sing it as a victory song against our enemy. We know it as truth despite the conflicting evidence we may now see in this realm of flesh.

We do not fear because we wield the living and powerful, two edged sword of the spirit that cuts through the fogs of confusion and pierces the darkness with his light (Genesis 1:18, John 1:4, Hebrews 4:12). It is able to discern secret thoughts and wicked intents and to bring them into submission. The word of God goes forth in victory and does not return void. We can trust His word to accomplish His purpose even when we are doubtful of our course and troubled by our circumstances. God's word will guide us and strengthen us as we advance toward our enemy. God will cause the obstacles of the enemy to serve his purpose and to bow to His will (Genesis 50:20, John 19:11, Romans 8:28). We are strong because we wield the truth and the facts as established in God's word. That great power will command our victory and give us our deliverance (Psalm 18:19, Acts 27:25). Through the power of His word, the Lord will dismiss the enemy assignment and establish His will and His kingdom.

✳ ROADSIDE REFLECTIONS:

- When you honestly assess your prowess and capability in handling scripture to achieve victory in your daily battles would you say that you tactfully weld the "sword of the Lord" or does your skill come closer to carrying a scriptural "pocket knife"?

7. Prayer- Ephesians 5:18

A second weapon that Paul introduces in this passage is the weapon of prayer and supplication in the Spirit. Scriptural accounts teach us that an effective prayer life is a powerful weapon for overcoming enemies (Psalm 6:9-10), for conquering death (2 Kings 4:1-36), for moving obstacles or hindrances (Matthew 17:20), and for bringing healing (James 5:16-18). Effective prayer was the only tool that could be used to cast out and defeat powerful demons (Mark 9:29) and when Jesus prayed over five (5) loaves of bread and two (2) little fishes God multiplied them and blessed them to exceed the needs of thousands of hungry people (Matthew 14:13-21).

Praying enables us to transact the will of God in the lives of those around us and allows the Holy Spirit to speak to our hearts and minds. It empowers us with wisdom from on high (James 1:5). Prayer draws upon the might of the most powerful God and establishes His will and His kingdom here on earth (Matthew 6:10, Daniel 4:35). It is in our personal prayer closet that we become aware of any sins that we need to confess or of any wrong doings that we need to make right. Uncovering and confessing these things allows us to walk with the Father more closely and to better do his will and prevents our enemy from using them as doorways for greater temptation (Matthew 6:12-13).

Praying in the Spirit allows the Holy Spirit to strengthen our weakness, to work out our inner turmoil, and to give us the correct words to intercede for ourselves and on behalf of others (Romans 8:26). When we pray through the Spirit, we can pray the mind of Christ and the will of God into the present circumstances without allowing our selfish desires and personal affinities or affections to interfere. Honestly laying out all of our concerns and cares before the Lord in prayer prevents us from the preoccupation of worry and fear (Philippians 4:6, 1 Peter 5:7). When we are still before he Lord and allow the Holy Spirit to lead us, he will provide the word and the issues that we need to present to the Father and lay at his feet.

Prayer is an interactive and reciprocal process whereby we can take our concerns and cares directly to the Lord, place our requests before Him, and then ask Him specifically to intercede on our behalf or on the behalf of others. Spending time with God in prayer allows us an opportunity to speak with Him as well as to listen to him. In prayer, God puts himself at the access of his children and in return, His children place themselves in submission to His will (Luke 11:2-4). As children of God, we can stand on the promises of His word and believe that we will receive all that we ask of Him when we come to Him in prayer (1John 5:14-15).

God gives us permission to come to Him boldly (James 4:2, Hebrews 4:15-16). It is His desire to bless us and to enlarge His kingdom and His power within us. He invites us to make our petitions known and to trust Him to provide. He is able to make every good blessing available to us and to meet our needs when we place our needs before Him in prayer (Matthew 7:7-11, John 15:16, James 1:17). Many times our needs go unmet and our desires unfulfilled simply because we have not humbled ourselves and gone to our Heavenly Father to ask for that which we desire or need from Him.

DEVELOPING PERSONAL SPIRITUAL DISCIPLINES

God has prepared each of us very well as members of His army. We are fully equipped with spiritual armor and with a shield of faith to protect and to strengthen us. We have weapons to stand our ground and to claim our territory, and to advance against the enemy and his army. However, the development of solid spiritual disciplines will be vital in our work as ambassadors for God's kingdom because our weapons will only be as effective as our proficiency and consistency in using them.

We are reminded by the apostle Paul that our armor is of no value as long as it remains safely stored within our foot locker. We must be diligent to put on each piece of our covering daily as we prepare to take our position on the frontlines. Each fearfully wonderful woman must assume her responsibility for developing the spiritual disciplines she needs to be the vital, contributing member of the Body of Christ that God has called her to be (Ephesians 4:22-24). Having a well-disciplined spiritual life will not only keep her alive on the battlefield but will also keep her attune to the will of God, aware of his leading, and replenished for ministry.

We have already learned that anyone desiring to follow Christ must be willing to forsake all and to enlist in a life of diligent service and hard work. Traveling through a world that is not our home and attending to the ministry of God's people can be exhausting. Many things will distract us, entangle us and fight for our attention. We may find ourselves weary and worn from attending to the needs of others if we do not first learn to attend to our own needs. While it is true that Christ's love for us compels us to reach out with the good news of the gospel, it is also true that we can only share that which we know to be true and we can only give from the resources contained within our individual storehouse. It is the duty of every ambassador to grow up into her calling and into her fullness in the Lord. Just as every soldier advances from boot camp or basic training to fuller assimilation, greater understanding of the mission and greater proficiency and skill, so must we likewise grow from being spiritual babies to becoming mighty ambassadors for God's kingdom (1 Corinthians 3:1-5, Ephesians 4:14).

The three foundational spiritual disciplines each fearfully wonderful woman needs to develop are: 1) Personal Bible study and reading, 2) Reflection, meditation and contemplation, and 3) An effective personal prayer life. The development of these three spiritual disciplines will require time, dedication and discipline. Just as any skilled pianist began her musical career with hour upon hour of running the scales and every gifted artist developed their talent through the use of yards of canvas and multiple tubes of oil paint; so it is with becoming proficient in the knowledge of the word and with personal spiritual growth.

It is vital for each fearfully wonderful woman of God to know at the beginning of her spiritual walk that if she is going to grow in Christ then she must learn the discipline of taking time to step away from the crowds in order to pray and to meditate and to study God's word. Each of us must desire to nurture our own intimate relationship with God above seeking ministry, title or position with the body of Christ. Christ must be our desire and our sufficiency. The word of God tells us to seek Him first and then all other things will be opened to us (Matthew 6:33). We should seek fellowship with God through Christ Jesus because of who He is and not because of what He gives.

We have already examined the value and importance of an effective prayer life as a weapon against our enemy as well as for the development of intimacy with God. Let's discuss the remaining disciplines of Bible reading and personal rumination or meditation.

THE DISCIPLINE OF PERSONAL BIBLE READING

At the most elementary level, the Bible is intended to be our guide book to lead us through this strange and sometimes difficult land in which we are now performing the duties of our King. It contains life giving truths, valuable tips for avoiding costly mistakes, and helpful insights to understanding the actions and attitudes of those around us. The Bible is still the number one best- selling book in the United States and probably holds the record for the most copies sold of any book in recorded history. A survey conducted by The Bible Society estimated that close to 6,000,000,000 copies translated into more than 2,000 languages and dialects had been produced through the year 1992. Over a decade later, The Bible still holds the number one spot on the list of the top ten best-selling books of all time (Ash, Russell, 2009). Based upon the present condition of our nation as well as that of the Church, one has to wonder how many of those Bibles were ever moved from the coffee table or the top shelf to the study desk or under the library reading lamp. A guide book that is not used to guide anyone anywhere is of no value. A Bible placed upon a library top shelf is not the equivalent of a Bible hidden in the heart of the one seeking to know God and to live life following His design. The Bible must be read and understood to be effective in a person's life.

DEVOTIONAL BIBLE READING

There are basically two distinct purposes for any Christian to approach reading their Bible. The first purpose is for devotional reading. We have already learned that a personal relationship requires that the people seeking such a relationship spend time together, develop a report, share insights, thoughts and opinions, and learn deeper personal things about one another.

No personal relationship can be established between two people who do not spend time together. The Bible also teaches us that we cannot be disciples of Jesus Christ if we do not have a time for regular study of the Word of God and of Christ's teachings. The Bible is vital for every Christian. We cannot grow spiritually or develop a closer walk with the Lord if we do not spend time becoming familiar with the Book in which He has made Himself known to us.

Devotional Bible reading is for the purpose of developing a deeper walk with the Lord and is focused on personal growth or on daily guidance and strength. It's also often a nice glance or the first approach to an area of interest before launching deeply into a more thorough study of that particular chapter, topic or character biography. Many people would consider their devotional time as the appetizer or the quick bite as opposed to being a main course or a four course sit-down meal. Listed below are some things to consider when developing the discipline of devotional Bible reading your life.

1. Choosing Time and Place

Most people set aside a particular block of time during a designated time of the day to sit before the Lord in devotional reading and prayer. Our lives are all different and our schedules vary but many fearfully wonderful women have reported that having their devotional time in the morning before the day's busyness begins helps them to focus and to center themselves and to start their day out right. Others enjoy quieting themselves and ending their day in the Lord's presence as they reflect over his blessings during the day. The time of the day in which you choose to establish your devotional time will be a personal decision.

Another factor to consider in establishing your devotional routine is to choose a private and quiet place in which to read, and pray. This needs to be a place where you will be free from distraction and where you can approach the Bible in an attitude of prayer and expectancy. Remember the purpose of this time is personal worship and prayer time. It is your opportunity to seek private fellowship with our Father and with Jesus Christ. It is during this time that God will meet with you and will reveal a truth to you as well as strengthen you for your day's ministry.

2. Choosing Materials

There are many ways to approach establishing a time for devotional reading. Some Christians choose a devotional reader written by an author they admire to guide their quiet time while others choose to read directly from the scripture. There are many books available that are dedicated to devotional reading and many websites will now email a daily devotional thought or scripture verse directly to your cell phone or office computer. Anyone interested should try out a few of the various resources to determine which style fits best for their personal needs. There are resources for individual devotions, family devotions and couples' devotions. There are devotional readers dedicated to particular seasons or holidays and devotionals for each of the life stages and varied ages through which we pass. Some fearfully wonderful women enjoy reading on a particular theme such as grace or love while others have devoted devotional time to studying the attributes and character of God or reading through the entire Bible one chapter at a time. Every ambassador should try several approaches to her devotional time and be willing to change approaches as well as resources as her life demands mandate. Flexibility and dedication will be key to faithfully practicing a devotional time.

PERSONAL BIBLE STUDY

We stated earlier that there are two distinct or separate purposes for a follower of Christ to utilize when approaching Bible reading. The first was that of developing a personal devotional time with the Lord through the reading of his word. The second spiritual discipline related to God's Word is the development of personal Bible study. Taking a few minutes each day for devotional time or to read a chapter or two is a good way to start to develop our discipline of Bible study ,but as we grow in our spiritual walk we should begin to block out extended periods of time beyond our devotional time to explore God's Word and to reflect upon what He is saying to us specifically through it. If we continue the analogy of our devotional time being our appetizer; then our personal Bible study is for the purpose of getting into the "meat" of God's word. We cannot grow in our knowledge of our faith or be empowered for our mission munching on appetizers alone. Growing bodies require adequate meals. We should each set aside a specific amount of time to study the word of God on a daily basis. We cannot count on our Pastor or the select ministers to whom we listen on the radio or television to provide us with all the Biblical knowledge that we will require to live a successful, thriving Christian life. It is our personal responsibility to develop our spiritual life and to grow in our depth of knowledge of the Lord Jesus Christ (2 Peter 3:18, 2 Timothy 2:15).

An obvious place to begin in personal Bile study is in the selection of a Bible translation that you can understand and that you enjoy reading. There are multiple versions and translations as well as many different styles and sizes available on the market today. While most people eventually end up with an assortment of various translations that contain different study tools such as maps, concordances and dictionaries; it's best to have at least one Bible that is written in the same translation that your minister or favorite teacher uses. This helps immensely in following along during worship service or in a study group. You may also want an additional paraphrased or modern translation for your devotional reading that might be easier for you to read and to understand. Remember, choosing a Bible is a purely personal thing. The most important factor is to choose one that you will enjoy reading and hence will be more likely to pick up and use.

Bibles can be purchased from a wide range of prices and most expensive doesn't always translate as the best choice. Prices will vary based upon cover materials, weight of paper and the number and type of study helps that a Bible includes. You may find that you do not need for the Bible that you use most often to contain a great number of extras such as a concordance, dictionary, foot notes or study guides. Remember that you can also purchase these references and tools separately at a lower price and begin to build a home study library that way. Be sure to check second hand book stores and church or seminary rummage sales for bargains. Also remember that many of these tools are available online and are often free of charge or at a minimal subscription service fee.

There is no one 'right' way to study the Bible. There are specific courses offered for learning how to study the Bible effectively by employing a variety of methods and by learning to utilize inductive and deductive reasoning. Browse a Christian bookstore for a study guide that appeals to you and try out a few to see which seems to fit your way of thinking best. You may even find that you can approach a passage of scripture utilizing multiple methodologies for deeper knowledge. Also, consider joining a group Bible Study. Many fearfully female scholars report that they learn more when they share thoughts with others or are lead by someone who is gifted as a Bible teacher. There are study groups based on age or sex as well as on specific topics of interest. Check local church bulletins as well as on-line resources, Bible schools and seminaries for courses being offered in your area. The bottom line is that finding a method that helps you approach the Bible with confidence and joy will be paramount to the development and sustainability of your desire and dedication to consistent personal study.

Some fearfully wonderful women improve their study time by keeping a journal or a notebook in which to write down questions or to jot quick notes from their reading. This discipline may help to remember questions to bring up later for answer or deeper exploration in study sessions with a small group or with your Pastor. Journaling and keeping study notes also helps to hone in on the key topics and central themes of particular biblical authors or books of the Bible. A simple way to begin this practice is to end each study session by writing down three (3) key notes that you learned from your reading. Notes can be used to find answers from other sources, to compare interpretations and insights from multiple sources and to share insights and findings with fellow ambassadors. Comparing journals from previous years of study is wonderful to remind us of how much we have grown , of what we have learned about our Lord and of how faithful and steadfast our shepherd has been in leading us in his instructions.

Other Ambassadors love to use differently colored pencils or highlighters to underscore specific passages, repeated words or central ideas contained in the text that they are studying. Some make notations in the margins of their Bible and list other Bible verses out to the side of the scripture that they are now studying to use as additional references. These "chained" verses serve as a guide to help in navigating more quickly from one verse to another and provide deeper insight and understanding to the topic of discussion. One well- known "chained" reference helps users guide others through the plan of salvation by beginning with John 3:16 and going step by step through several verses within the book of Romans. Any fearfully wonderful woman of God could custom design her own chained references on the topic of her choosing with a little due diligence.

Any fearfully wonderful woman of God who sincerely desires to develop the habit of consistent daily Bible study should begin by making her Bible study time as comfortable and as beneficial as possible. She should consider what materials she would like to have available and talk with other fearfully wonderful women about the tools and tips that they incorporate into their personal study. For example, she may want to purchase a zippered or snapped Bible cover that will not only protect the soft leather exterior of her Bible but also hold a journal, pens and sticky notes securely together with her chosen Bible translation.

✖ ROADSIDE REFLECTIONS:

- What is your favorite method for studying the Bible? Do you incorporate any of the ideas discussed within your routine? Are there any of these that you are willing to try? Are there other methods or tools that you use that could be added to the provided list?

BIBLICAL SCHOLARSHIP AND MINISTRY

Bible study is about more than the mere accumulation of facts and knowledge and regardless of the various methods that ambassadors of God's kingdom choose to employ to study His word, it is important to remember that the Bible is unlike any other book available to human kind. Though it holds a great deal of historical record and pertinent information, it must not be approached as a source of academic information or cultural history alone. The Bible alone is the inspired and living word of Almighty God. It holds the key to abundant life now, eternal life forevermore, and to overflowing blessing and joys beyond our capacity to comprehend or to measure. The Bible is to be approached as a living and supernatural document offering insight and providing counsel from God on matters of importance to Him. We study the Bible to acquire wisdom and to enhance our relationship with the Almighty God of the universe not to simply earn a diploma or another charm for our spiritual bracelet. Our Father's living word can be a source of *inspiration* and *illumination* as well as an index of guidance and instruction for *application* to our personal lives. Reading and applying God's word to our heart, mind and soul provides the *transformation* of our being into a closer replication of all that God intended. A strong Biblical foundation will be the principal source of encouragement and strength for our own Christian walk as well as for the lives of those who walk with us.

- **Inspiration**

New Christians and long- time followers of Christ alike can appreciate the Bible as a source of *inspiration*. Reading the gospel accounts of the life and ministry of our leader, Jesus Christ can help us to better understand our mission and inspire us to follow in his footsteps. New Ambassadors can apply the lessons learned by those who traveled for the gospel before us to their current life situations. We can gain a better understanding of what it means to live a life of faith by examining the Biblical accounts of those heroes and heroines who lived such lives before us and left us their examples (Hebrews 11: 1-39). Teaching Bible stories to our children from an early age is a vital tool for inspiring them to be great men and women of God as well. Encouraging our children to memorize and to recite scripture verses will help them hide away words of truth or encouragement to be used when they are tempted to be disobedient, unkind or otherwise naughty. Committing scripture to memory to call upon in times of temptation will provide protection by keeping these little ones from falling prey to sin (Psalm 119:11).

- **Illumination**

We can also refer to the Bible as a source of *illumination* or for greater insight and clarity of understanding. Looking into God's word will often " shed light" on a gray area in our life or offer greater discernment related to an issue that isn't quite settled in our hearts and minds. Reading God's Word helps us to understand more about our creator and about His design plan for His creation and for our eternal being. The truths contained in the Bible shed light upon God's character and give us a historical reference for His various covenants, ordinances and laws. Examining the context and historical timeline of His interactions with various people throughout Biblical history will heighten our understanding of God's continued interactions with various people groups today. Present day followers can chronicle God's kept promises with mankind; beginning with Adam and leading to the fulfillment of the delivery of the promised Messiah. Gaining such insight into the character and attributes of the nature of our God will help us know His heart and in turn trust His love for us. It is at this stage of study that an ambassador might consider investing in additional study tools such as various concordances and commentaries as well as a good Bible dictionary.

- **Application and Transformation**

Sooner or later in our Christian walk we realize that simply reading the Bible is not enough to sustain a victorious and thriving Christian life. As we grow in our faith, we must move from simple inspiration and illumination to personal *application*. When we are no longer babies in the faith, we are required to practice what we have read and to be doers of the Word rather than mere listeners (James 1:19-25, Matthew 7:21).

Those of us who sincerely desire to fulfill God's will and purpose will not only read His word but will be open to his leading and instruction regarding the specific application of its content to our individual lives. Applying the principles set forth in the scripture is the cohesive that binds us together as one body in faith and in fellowship (Ephesians 5:19, Hebrews 10:23-32). It is what sets us apart as a distinctive people who serve the same God and recognize the authority of Christ Jesus (1Peter 2:9).We must ask the Holy Spirit to illuminate the scriptures to us as we contemplate the deeper meanings and meditate upon the passages that we read. We must allow his Holy Spirit to speak to us and to show us areas in which we may need to change our conduct or our attitude in light of what we have read. In this manner, the *application* of God's word that is directed by the *illumination* of the Holy Spirit will produce the *transformation* of our old natures into the changed image of our new self that more fully reflects and glorifies Christ (2 Corinthians 3:16-18, Galatians 5:16-18). Jesus was able to resist and to ultimately defeat the enemy not because he merely knew scripture but because he lived it and relied upon it for instruction and empowerment.

- **Encouraging others**

Scripture instructs us to encourage and to disciple others by teaching them to observe God's commands (Matthew 28:18-20). At the ministry level, fearfully wonderful women of God should place teaching new Christians as well as our own children the truth of God's Word among our top priorities. After all, having a working knowledge of God's word will be their protection against false teachers who may twist or otherwise change the message of God's word and seek to lead them astray (Matthew 7:15, Jeremiah 23:16. Knowing the truths of God's promises will provide a solid foundation upon which to stand when they are facing times of difficulty and pain (Jeremiah 1:12, Psalms 1:1-3, Psalm 77:1-3, 2 Peter 1:4).

Logically, we cannot instruct others in knowing how to lead victorious Christian lives or in how to be obedient to God's instructions, if we are not familiar with the keys to overcoming our enemy and to living a spirit lead life for ourselves (2 Corinthians 3:6,2 Timothy 2:15). We cannot teach what we do not know. We cannot give what we do not have. If we want to follow God more closely and to instruct others, then we must know what His word says. Mentoring, teaching or discipling others is a position that is not to be taken lightly. God's word has repeated cautions for those who lead others astray by teaching falsehood (Luke 17:2, 1 Timothy 4, Hebrews 5:10-12). We must be able to draw upon our own personal knowledge of the scripture in ministry to fellow believers. Our ignorance cannot be an excuse for sharing incorrect information.

The Apostle Paul instructs believers to let the word of Christ dwell in us richly as we teach and admonish one another (Colossians 3:16). Scripture is the only path to learning who Jesus is and to presenting the plan of salvation to others (1 John 1:14, John 3:16, Romans 3:23). Scripture is also available to us as we encourage one another to walk closely to Jesus (Romans 15:4), to be motivated to give Christ our best (Philippians 4:8) and to encourage and strengthen as well as to comfort one another (1 Thessalonians 5:14, 2 Thessalonians 2:17). We must be certain as ministering ambassadors that we have a personal comfort with our Bibles that includes an ease in finding verses within the body of the Bible as well as with quoting scripture. We also need to be able to explain how a particular scripture applies to present situation. If we are clumsy or insecure in our knowledge and use of the scripture then we may not be able to access what is readily available to us in helping another in their time of need.

Memorizing and being able to recite scripture is a vital tool for spiritual warfare. Paul reminded us of the importance of the Sword of the Word of God as an offensive weapon for holding back our enemy and his armies. He told us that the Word of God is the chief weapon that God has given us to defeat him (Ephesians 6:17, 1 John 4:4-6). It is when we study scripture and know it and can call upon its truth that we abolish Satan's lies, bring his arguments captive and establish the truth of Christ (2 Corinthians 10:5, Matthew 4:4-10). We cannot claim our birth-right nor walk in our authority if we do not know the contents of our inheritance or covenant with God.

Scripture reading is important in warfare because reading the biblical accounts of his prior workings makes us keenly aware of Satan's previous tactics and schemes, cunning and practices (1 Peter 5:8, 1 Corinthians

10:12, John 8:44, Isaiah 14:12-15, 2 Corinthians 4:4). We cannot expect to be victorious over our enemy, either as individuals or as the Body of Christ, if we have not studied him or if we know nothing about his tactics. Through scripture, we can be forewarned of the tools and devises that he will seek to use against us and of what activities or "fruits" indicate that he may be at work among us (1 John 2:16, Galatians 5:19-21.

✖ ROADSIDE REFLECTIONS:

- What academic grade would you assign yourself for Biblical scholarship and scripture memorization? What are some steps that you can take to improve those areas of your life?

- Does the Word of God inspire, illuminate and transform your daily life?

GET ME TO A MONASTERY?

Practicing the spiritual discipline of meditation does not require the seclusion of a monastery or even that we wear robes or be able to chant. Neither should it be a ritualized routine that is reserved for a select cloistered and segregated few. A careful review of the scripture should remove all the mystery and hyper-spirituality from the practice of meditation and reveal that this discipline needs to be an integral part of any growing or deepening walk with the Lord. Practically speaking, meditation is the natural extension of an effective prayer life and as such should be the habitual practice of each of us who is seeking to know God and to follow His will.

The Psalmist declared in Psalm 119:12-16 that he would recount all God's laws, rejoice in his statutes, meditate on his precepts and delight in his decrees. The word for meditate as used in verse fifteen (15) is translated by Zodhiates to mean: "to converse with oneself out loud over, or to muse or speak" (Zodhiates, (1994), pp.115, pp. 2430).

In Philippians 4:8, Paul instructs believers to "think on" things that are just, true, pure and right. In his New Testament word study Zodhiates uses the original Greek word '*logizomai*' for the words "think on" as used in Philippians 4:8 and translates that word to mean : "to take an inventory of, to reason or reckon , or to suppose" (Zodhiates, (1991),pp.45). Based upon these few scriptural references and the word studies of Zodhiates, to mediate is to simply spend time thinking about, contemplating, musing over and internalizing God's precepts, laws and statues. It is focusing on the justice, goodness, honesty and virtue of His character.

The Psalmist stated that he would not neglect a single word of God's precepts and statues and that he was hiding God's word in his heart (Psalm 119:11). He stated that he was practicing all the disciplines that he outlined in order to keep his way pure (Psalm 119:9). Paul outlined a list of things upon which we were to contemplate in Philippians stating that these were the only things that were deserving of our praise and attention (Philippians 4:8). We can conclude from this scriptural introduction that the immediate benefit of mediation is that it keeps us pure. It is a defense against sin. Having scripture to call upon is a deterrent to satisfying the desires of the flesh and from eating the tempting fruits of the enemy (Galatians 5:19-21).

Just as our car operates and draws its power from the gasoline or fuel that we supply to its tank; it is true that we become what we think and that the meditations of our hearts are fundamentally connected to the words of our mouth and the actions of our bodies (Matthew 7:20-23, Psalm 19:14). It is from the wellspring of our hearts and minds that our mouth speaks and our physical being reacts (Matthew 15:18, Proverbs 4:23). If the content and substance of our hearts and minds is God's Word then we cannot help but be obedient to it. Meditating upon God's word and hiding it in our hearts brings our flesh into obedience and gives life to our spiritual being (Deuteronomy 30:19, 1Timothy 4:8).

We can conclude from these passages that meditation is a beneficial and practical discipline that every fearfully wonderful woman of God should seek to develop (Exodus 13:9, Psalm 71:17, and Psalm 78:4). However, there are a few very important distinctions that must be made between "New Age" or transcendental and other forms of mediation and the type of meditation that scripture encourages.

The first distinction that must be made is that all Christian mediation must be centered and focused on the truth of God's Word (Deuteronomy 6:7-8, Deuteronomy 11:18, 2 Timothy 2:7, Joshua 1:8). Christians need to be very cautious and avoid opening themselves up to practices that originate in pagan religious rituals such as guided imagery, focused journaling, chanting, dream interpretation and several other techniques being proposed within our secular culture as aides to effective meditation. There are many Biblical instructions warning us against witchcraft, divination and seeking counsel or wisdom from those who worship false gods (Deuteronomy 18:: 9-12, Isaiah 8:19, 1 Samuel 15:26-28). Even joining something as seemingly innocent as an exercise class based in yoga or deep breathing could open a Christian up to ungodly spiritual influences. The writing of the Psalmist and that of the Apostle Paul make it very clear that we are to set our focus on heavenly things and to seek counsel from God alone. Exercises and techniques that seem harmless may open a gateway to demonic oppression or other ungodly influences (1 Samuel 28).

For the Christian, mediation is the discipline of taking the time needed to step away from our life distractions to refocus our attention to our Lord or to his precepts and teaching. Meditation time can be used to simply think on the character and nature of our God and to extol his name to our physical being. We can meditate on how loving and gracious, steadfast and faithful our Father is to all his children. Meditation time could also be a time used to examine what we have recently read from God's word, to consider active ways in which it could specifically be applied to us, and then to perhaps commit it to memory so that we might call it out to our Lord or to speak it against our enemy. As we meditate, we must remember to ask God to give us wisdom to understand His truth and His desired application of the scripture. He promises to give wisdom freely to anyone who asks it of Him (James 1:5).

There is a second warning that must be offered to those fearfully wonderful women wishing to participate in Christian meditation. When Christians meditate upon the Word of God, we want to avoid presenting a blank mind or an open door to our enemy. This can be very dangerous as we have already learned what a battleground our mind can become. When we meditate we want to purposely focus our thinking, concentrate on the words of scripture and fill our minds completely with the Word of God. We want to quiet our bodies, hearts and minds as we allow the Holy Spirit to teach us the deeper meanings of God's promises and instructions to us. When we enter into our private prayer closets to seek out a time for meditation we want to begin with a prayer inviting God to come and commune with us and to guide our thoughts during this time. We also want to recognize His sovereignty and to ask His protection. We want to openly dedicate this time to worship and adoration of Him. If we have any stray thoughts we want to immediately bring those captive and place them before the Lord. We need to hide ourselves in the shadow of the Almighty and be very aware that the enemy will seek to distract us, to block communication and to disable our prayer and study time just as he sought to interrupt and to tempt Jesus as He prayed in the Garden of Gethsemane (Luke 22:49-54) .

✳ ROADSIDE REFLECTIONS:

- Did you ever consider that resting before the Lord is actually a spiritual discipline? Yes. Being still is much like fasting as it removes our thoughts from distractions, busyness and other things of lesser importance and helps us to focus on the presence of the Lord and to hear what He might say to us. Is resting and meditating a spiritual discipline that you need to incorporate into your life? What are some steps that you might take to develop this discipline?

- Is your spiritual gas tank running on empty? Does your life need a spiritual tune up?

CHAPTER 11

Choosing Our Traveling Companions

How many countless tubes of pink lipstick can be found on any given day within your favorite cosmetics department? That "pink" lipstick may actually be labeled as petal, peony, petunia, and palest or passionate. Its color may be identified as bridal, burgundy, berry or bubblegum. Lipstick can come in a tube, a pot, a crayon or with its own little wand. It can be sheer, matte, glossy, translucent, wet, shimmering or long lasting with all day staying power. Yet, if we remove all the fancy packaging and strip away the variable names and advertising what do we have? A pink lipstick by any other name is still… a pink lipstick. It is at its core a cosmetic designed to add a little color and moisture to a person's mouth.

So it is with defining the word "woman" or in seeking to capture the essence of what it means to be "female" or a "fearfully wonderful woman of God". There are as many variations on the concept of female and the feminine as there are pink lipsticks at the L'Oreal counter.

Becoming a fearfully wonderful woman of God is not about fitting into someone else's rigid definitions or stereotypes. Fearful females and wonderful women know who they are and are comfortable in their own skin. They each bear the fingerprint of their creator- the original designer label- and recognize that they are truly a unique individual and a one of a kind creation. These wonderful women also recognize that just as "pink" lipsticks can be slightly different in hue, formula or packaging so can their sisters who travel with them. Each fearfully wonderful woman of God has learned to cherish and to respect the unique beauty of herself and of her sisters. As women of God on the journey of life together, we must allow for the freedom to display varied personal characteristics, styles, callings, passions, talents and giftings. This is how we become fitted together as the Body of Christ (Ephesians 4:11-16).

❊ ROADSIDE REFLECTIONS:

- As we begin to examine our relationships with fellow sojourners, there are three words over which I am puzzling. How you think these three words are inter-related and how do they apply to our interaction within our relationships with each other and with God?

- Relationship

- Respect

- Responsibility

- How colorful is the tapestry composed of your various friendships? Do you branch out to include women who are different from you in terms of educational attainment, financial status, social position or age within your entourage of friends?

DEVELOPING AN ENCOURAGEMENT ENTOURAGE

What an absolute pleasure it is to be in the company of fearfully wonderful women of God who have truly embraced the joy found in knowing the freedom to be themselves. These women can roll down a hill, run barefoot in the grass, wear red cowboy boots, and paint their toenails bright pink. They dare to paint outside the lines using a color that was not identified as the correct one in the paint by number instructions. They are unashamed in lifting their hands in total abandon in worship to the Lord and will say amen when moved by a word or a song. They have learned that where the Spirit of the Lord is there is total freedom (2 Corinthians 3:17). These women stand fast in the Liberty that Christ won for them and boldly display their love of the Lord and of each other (Galatians 5:1).

Fearfully wonderful women of God can be imperfect and are unafraid to allow others to see their flaws and to minister to their needs. They will invite you in for coffee, call you just to say that they are thinking of you, laugh along with your silliness, and tell you the truth when your pants really do make your rear end appear larger than it is. These women can laugh at the day ahead knowing that they are loved unconditionally by a Father who knows them as they really are and takes great pleasure in calling them "Daughter" (Proverbs 31:25, Zephaniah 3:10). Their security is found in knowing that He will provide all their needs and answer each of their prayers. These are the women we need to seek out as our traveling companions.

Such women are our fabulously free sisters in the body of Christ. They are women who are anchored in the love of their Lord and unafraid to be touched by humanity's suffering and pain. They will bear your sorrow, encourage your faith and call you out on your grumbling and complaining. These women make the best members of any encouragement entourage. Be certain that you not only seek out such women as your traveling companions but that you also make it your earnest prayer and heart's desire to be such a woman in the lives of your sisters. Because, like it or not, your mother was correct when she told you that in order to have friends you must first be a friend. Friendships will not grow up spontaneously and we will not establish connections with other women if we cannot allow ourselves to be vulnerable, and risk their rejection by confirming our desire to be a friend.

Friendships can spring up in the most unusual places and oftentimes our dearest friends start out as people whom we would never have considered to be our friends at all due to our lack of common backgrounds or shared interests. If we can trust God to lead in the process of bringing others into our lives and can allow ourselves to move beyond our insecurities and prejudices to embrace sisters in the Lord that are slightly different then wonderful bonds of friendship can occur. Our differences can actually be an enrichment to the relationship and offer a chance to expand our perspectives and interests. Being open to a relationship with a sister who is of a different culture, race, denomination, generation or social background may lead to a life changing friendship. Our Father knows our gifting and our short comings. He knows our stage of spiritual development. He knows our specific needs in terms of which people will challenge us or nurture us, and thereby strengthen our spiritual growth and development. God knows who best among our sisters will be " iron sharpening our iron" and will help to mold us into an honorable vessel fit for his service (Proverbs 27:17, 2 Timothy 2:21, Ephesians 2:10). When our loving Father does establish

His God-given and anointed friendships in our lives they are like none other and should be valued and treasured. Such friends are an invaluable expression of the love of God and are grounded and rooted in true love that originates with Him (John 13:35, 1 John 4:8).

While it is true that it is God who establishes relationships; all fearfully wonderful women of God need to pray to be more sensitive to the Holy Spirit's leading and more open to opportunities to be a friend in the lives of those around us. It is far too easy to become ingrained in our own routines and to hastily run along in life without stopping to think about, pray for or respond to the needs of those other women within our churches, neighborhoods or communities. Friendships with our sisters must be sought out and then they must be nurtured and maintained. A quick phone call, short email or hug as we pass in the doorway will go a long way to brighten the day of our sisters who are often just as busy and just as frazzled as we. May we all learn to be more obedient to the nudges of the Holy Spirit and respond more quickly when He places a sister's name on our hearts. Sharing such openness and vulnerability in the Lord will strengthen our unity in Christ and encourage each of our individual walks.

Dear Old Mom was also correct when she wouldn't allow you to associate with someone with disagreeable manners or with the girl at school who had a questionable reputation. She probably told you that she wouldn't allow your friendship for fear that those other people would be a bad influence on you. Your mother may have told you that a person is known by the company that they keep or that " birds of a feather flock together". The wisdom of the Bible would agree with your mother in proclaiming that: "we are who we hang out with". 1Corinthians 15:33 warns us: *Do not be misled: "Bad company corrupts good character"* and Proverbs 13:20 states that *"the companion of fools suffers harm"*. The Lord wants each of us as his daughter to carefully choose our friends while we are on this earth (Proverbs 12:26). Choosing friends who are like minded and who share our faith will help to keep us rooted and grounded and filled with the fullness of God (Ephesians 3:17-19). Being in the company of Christian friends will hold us accountable to produce a life in which our thoughts, actions and communications are pleasing to God. When we walk with wise people we will begin to grow in wisdom ourselves (Proverbs 13:20). Likewise our faith cannot grow and we cannot mature in our walk with the Lord if we allow ourselves to be unequally yoked together with unbelievers (2 Corinthians 6:14).

If we are seeking to honor the Lord and to be all that he created us to be, why in the world would we desire the company of those who will not benefit our efforts? We cannot soar with the eagles if we flock with the turkeys. We cannot continue to fellowship with those who set their hearts on the things of this world if we are striving to be more like Christ (2 Corinthians 6:17). As we surrender our lives to God's sovereign Lordship, we must trust his guidance and allow Him to establish new friendships while he perhaps calls us to end others. He will begin to prune out the people that He does not want in our lives and to bring alongside those people that He does want us to join with in our journey.

Seeking out an encouragement entourage composed of those sisters who will build us up in our faith does not mean that we cannot be sensitive to the needs of those around us or offer hospitality and kindness to our coworkers and neighbors who need to find Christ. The good news of the gospel compels us to share his message of grace and salvation with everyone. Remember we are ambassadors on a heavenly mission. We are Jesus' only hands and voice within the world today. As such, we need to have his eyes and his heart in our interactions and dealings with those who do not yet know him and so desperately need him. Jesus came to offer relationship with God to those who were considered social outcasts. He ate with tax collectors and prostitutes. But when Jesus spoke with the lost or ate with those of ill repute it was with the express purpose of presenting a way of redemption and restitution. He pointed out their sin and offered them hope. He never winked at sinful transgressions or tolerated compromise or incomplete repentance. Recall that the rich young ruler went away unchanged when he found our Lord's requirements too stringent (Luke 18:18-23). Jesus never lowered his standards or altered his beliefs to fit in or to gain the approval of the masses. He presented the truth of the gospel and then allowed each individual to make their own decision to accept or to reject His teaching. When He left the earth He commissioned us to do exactly as He had done and to present the gospel truth to everyone (Matthew 28:18-20). His parting words are still a vital part of our kingdom business today. As ambassadors of God's kingdom, we need to constantly seek out ways to reach out to the lost and to be hospitable to all with whom we come in contact but we need to be careful that we do not compromise our beliefs or make ungodly alliances with unbelievers (Exodus 34:12-14). All fearfully wonderful women of God want to be certain that our closest friends and most trusted allies are those women who will encourage us and strengthen our walk. Sharing a common acknowledgement of Jesus

Christ as our Lord contributes a deep and loving bond in friendships that is unlike any other. That is because Christ is the core and the anchor of such relationships and it is His enduring love that flows through us and that establishes our loyalty and commitment to each other (Ecclesiastes 4:12).

⁂ ROADSIDE REFLECTIONS:

- Who are the members of your encouragement entourage? What are the qualities and strengths of each person that lead you to invite them to come alongside you on life's journey?
- What qualities do you possess that make you a valuable friend and member of an encouragement entourage?
- Do you have some traveling companions with whom you possibly need to limit interaction or to part company with altogether?

ON BEING CHEERLEADERS, CONFIDANTS AND COACHES

Our God is a God of order and in following His example we must live our lives in an orderly fashion and establish clearly defined boundaries and limitations within our relationships with one another. Every relationship demands a choice. As Christians we must not be passive in our relationships with others. We must be an active participant and not allow ourselves to become a hapless victim or an apathetic or uninvolved spectator. To keep our friendships healthy and vital each friend should begin the new relationship by being clear about values and life goals, time constraints and responsibilities. Honesty sincerely is the best policy. Friends must openly discuss how they imagine this relationship will operate within their current set of constraints. In speaking the truth in love, we must define the purpose and direction of each of our friendships. We must establish boundaries in our relationships and then hold ourselves and our friends accountable to them. When a friend has overstayed her welcome, becomes too dependent upon us or is taking up too much of our time and is perhaps keeping us from accomplishing our daily chores or doing those things that we know that the Lord has called us to do we must speak the truth in love. Friendships that are out of balance or too demanding can quickly become little foxes eating away at our time and taking away from our other responsibilities (Song of Solomon 2:15). Time that should be devoted to our personal spiritual growth and ministry or to the care and nurturing of our family can be eaten up by friendships that are operating without healthy limitations.

Friendship is an awesome gift from God that carries a high level of responsibility. True friendship cannot occur without reciprocity, open sharing and communication, commitment to each other and to the relationship, and mutual respect. Friends need to be honest with each other about their expectations for their relationship. If we are fearful in expressing our needs as well as our limitations to our friends, then our relationships are not based in truth or operating in Christian love (1 John 4:18).Without carefully and clearly defined expectations friendships can quickly become one sided, co-dependent, possessive and unhealthy. Psychologist and author, John Townsend, has stated repeatedly in much of his writing that friendships without boundaries lead to emotional and spiritual distress and struggle. He states that it is virtually impossible to love properly without boundaries and that balanced relationships are only established where both truth and love are equally present (Townsend, 1991). A few indications that a relationship is operating without proper boundaries in place include going against one's personal values or rights to please the other, allowing the other to take as much as they can get from us, letting the other direct our life, letting the opinion of the other define us, and failing to notice when the other has invaded our life and displayed inappropriate behaviors (Cloud and Townsend, 1992).

Truthfulness on our part requires being willing to risk rejection or the chance that someone else will not become our friend if we are open about our particular needs and about how we see a potential friendship meeting those needs in our life at this time. We must carefully outline and explain what we seek in a friendship being honest about our emotional, psychological and spiritual expectations. We must also be honest in disclosing just how much time and energy we presently have to devote to a friendship. If one person's needs are greater than the other person's capacity to give then it would be best to avoid hurt feelings, jealousy and disappointment by opting out of a close friendship at this time.

True friends desire to encourage each other towards faithful and obedient service to our Lord. We are sensitive to each other's needs and seek to be a source of comfort and support to one another; we love one another and bear one another's burdens (Galatians 6:2-5). As sisters we are called to be cheerleaders, confidants and coaches in one another's lives and to respond to one another with grace and patience (1 Corinthians 13:4). We are instructed to identify with one another's hardships and to share one another's pain; however, scripture does not call us to become professional counselors or spiritual mediators in the lives of our friends and nowhere are we encouraged to nurse one another's bitterness, unforgiveness or rebellion and sin. While each ambassador of God's kingdom shares the co-laboring responsibility of praying, speaking the truth in love and waiting for the Spirit of God to work in our sister's hearts; ministering to one another in true intercession and friendship will require that we be able to discern when to be personally available to our sisters and when to suggest that they seek out the counsel of their pastor or perhaps even someone in a professional counseling capacity.

Our friendship and love for our sisters will cause us to want to pray with and for them as well as to speak godly counsel and truth into their lives. We must, however, never allow our influence in our sisters' lives to become a substitute for their reliance upon the Lord. True ministry that is guided by godly love for our sisters requires that we be cautious not to "help" them too much. If we are overprotective or overly mothering we may interfere in the work of the Lord in their lives. As ambassadors of His kingdom, we must be careful to be sensitive to the will of the Lord in the life of our sister and to seek to know his heart and to understand what changes and growth he is trying to bring about within her.

One area that can be particularly challenging for fearfully wonderful women of God is that of keeping secrets for others. Intercessors are often called into confidence by their sisters. However, keeping secrets in the Body of Christ can be a divisive and damaging thing to do. We want to be certain before we pledge our confidence that keeping our sister's secret will not force us to have to lie to others or drive a wedge in our relationships with others.

Often our sisters will come to us with a "prayer request" or a confession and ask that we not share the information with anyone else. When a sister seeks to call us into her confidence or asks us to keep a secret we need to be careful that we do not hinder her relationship with God by allowing her to harbor or hide an unconfessed sin or secret habit, or to secretly live in a sinful manner. To do so would be detrimental to her spiritual walk. We also want to be certain that her secret is not placing her physical or emotional well-being in jeopardy. Our natural empathy and desire to love and to nurture our sisters in the Lord cannot become safety nets and barriers that prevent them from falling on God's grace and calling out for his strong arm of salvation and redemption. Our secret keeping cannot be a substitute for leading her to confess her sin and to ask God to forgive and to cleanse her. God has promised to forgive us but only after we come to Him and openly confess (1 John 1:9-10). Allowing others to really know her and confessing her sin openly while casting all her care upon the Lord will lead to greater spiritual growth and happiness (James 5:26, 1 John 1:19-20, 1 Peter 5:7). If we have learned anything from the story of Adam and Eve is that our sinful nature desires to hide our sin once we have committed it rather than to expose it and to ask for forgiveness. The weight of hidden or unconfessed sin can quickly become an overwhelming burden and a stumbling block to intimacy with God.

✖ ROADSIDE REFLECTIONS:

- How do we know when keeping a secret for someone or sharing a prayer request with another has crossed over into a gray area or become an avenue for sin to enter into a relationship? How can we avoid such situations?

- Psalm 15:1-3, Proverbs 6:19 and Ecclesiastes 10:20 are a few of the verses that I use to check myself regarding gossip or slander. Are there others that you might add to the list?

- In James 2:8-13 we are warned against taking position and authority in others' lives that belong to God alone. How do we balance our desire to help and to counsel others with staying out of God's way in the process? In what ways might we be guilty of "playing god" in the lives of others through our desire to minister?

CRIPPLING COMPASSION

Those of us who are in a position of ministry, as well as any fearfully wonderful woman with an altruistic and empathetic nature, must be careful to avoid falling into the trap of extending our compassion and love for our sister beyond the point of benefiting her spiritual, emotional and physical well-being and growth. Often times a person needs to come to the end of their self- reliance and social support network before they are humble enough to ask anything from the Lord (Proverbs 16:18, James 4:10). Your sister may be desperately clinging to your gentle support because she has not yet reached out to God as her all sufficient provider (Isaiah 40). She may be overly dependent upon your friendship because she has not met "the friend that sticketh closer than a brother" and the one who will never leave her or forsake her (Proverbs 18:24, Matthew 28:20). We do our sisters no service if we allow our "help" to prevent them from learning the faithfulness of God's character and the steadfast assurance of His promises (Isaiah 55:6, 58:9, Jeremiah 33:3). She could have no greater friend than Jesus to carry her through times of trial or tribulation (Psalm 56:3, John 15:13).

Discipling another women within the body of Christ is an awesome opportunity to see the work of God within another person's life as we co-labor together with Him. It becomes vitally important in such mentoring relationships that we model respect and teach responsibility. When discipling or mentoring another fearfully wonderful woman of God we must sincerely value and respect her opinions and her personal relationship with the Lord. We need to be careful not to treat her as if she cannot make spiritual decisions without us or cannot hear the voice of the Lord unless we interpret or guide her. We also want to be certain that each of us respects the margins and barriers that have been established in our relationship. If our mentoring relationship is not built upon mutual respect and individual responsibility then our interactions can lead our sister to develop an unhealthy dependence upon us and can quench our sister's desire to seek out the counsel of the Lord for herself. Fearfully wonderful women of God must not allow others to vicariously follow the Lord by following us. Christian friendship and ministry cannot be sustained through the establishment of cliques or fan clubs. True friends want their sisters to commit their lives to the Lord's keeping and to follow Him in service. It should never be our desire to create a clone of ourselves in those whom we have the privilege to mentor or to lead. Their individual Christian walk cannot simply mimic or duplicate our walk and we must not allow them to trust their spiritual growth to our responsibility. We must dissuade our sisters against committing themselves to us in undying friendship or as a loyal member of our fan base. Fearfully wonderful women of God are careful to always point others to Jesus as the only source of life, freedom, and deliverance from the bondage of sin. As teachers, mentors, ministers and true friends we bear the responsibility to always point our sisters to Christ and to encourage them to seek him as their counselor in Chief and the source of all life giving wisdom. No minister of God's grace and love can allow herself to be placed upon a pedestal. Ambassadors of God's kingdom desire that all glory be given to Him alone in our ministry to others (1 Corinthians 10:31). We must be certain that our sisters' relationship with God is the only one in which she worships and deifies her friend.

⌘ ROADSIDE REFLECTIONS:

- What are some practical steps that we can take in ministering as Fearfully Wonderful women of God to avoid creating fan clubs, reproducing clones and crippling another sister's walk with the Lord through our misplaced or over extended compassion?

Holding on to Friendships Beyond their Expiration Date

"And He is before all things and by him all things consist"- Colossians 1:17

Friendships truly are the milk of life; for a true friendship, as the once popular United Dairy Farmers Association slogan declared: "does a body good". According to scripture, friendship sweetens our life and sharpens our walk (Proverbs 27:9-17) and laughing with a friend brings us health right down to the core of our being (Proverbs 17:22). True friends love us at all times despite our multitude of imperfections and short comings (Proverbs 17:17, 1 Peter 4:8). Having a friend to bear our burden lightens our load and when friends unite together in strength or agreement it becomes virtually impossible for any enemy to overtake or defeat them (Ecclesiastes 4:12). But just like milk, friendships often have an expiration date. Holding on to friendships or milk beyond that expiration date can sometimes result in some pretty negative consequences including being left with a bad taste in our mouths. Soured or curdled milk may be great for baking as well as in other recipes but if we take a big swig of soured milk right out of the jug our stomachs will turn and we will quickly spew it from our lips. Holding on to the tattered shreds of relationships that have outlived their purpose in God's plan and are now being propped up by our rationalizations, fear, guilt or apathy will have the same effect on our disposition and our attitude. Soured relationships produce sour people.

Everything that God creates has boundaries (Job 38:8-11). He made the sea to stop at the shore. He ordered the light of day to give way to the cover of night's darkness and the sun must surrender its reign in the heavens to the moon at the appointed time. All of life ends in death and there is a season for every purpose under heaven (Ecclesiastes 3:1-10). These words denoting structure and purpose in God's relationship with His creation also apply to the life and to the relationships of every fearfully wonderful woman of God. As previously discussed, healthy relationships can only exist within the confines of clearly defined and respected boundaries. One such boundary may be the boundary of time. Our creator has appointed the times and seasons of our lives. If we recognize Him as our Sovereign Lord, then it is He who must be allowed to orchestrate our relationships' beginnings as well as their endings.

While it is often difficult to know when it is time to let go of a friend or to allow a relationship to end, as we progress in life's journey and move in and out of various seasons and situations there will be people of whom we will have to let go in order to move forward. There are multiple reasons for terminating a friendship or for allowing a friendship to wane. Moving away from a particular town or city is an obvious example. Long distance relationships can be difficult to maintain and will often times dwindle away to an occasional email , the annual family newsletter, and of course, a Christmas card. Sometimes becoming a Christian can put an end to a friendship. Our new faith in the Lord may require leaving old friends behind. Friends can naturally drift apart when the shared interests or common ground that produced the friendship comes to an end. An example would be making friends with someone who has a child taking the same ballet class or playing on the same soccer team as your son or daughter. Often the end of the class or of the sports season means the end of the shared interest and the friendship.

Even Christian friends can part company when there is a call to a new ministry, a new church or a new life goal placed upon one of the friends that is not shared by the other. Learning to set one another free will allow each friend to grow in grace and in our walk with the Lord. Recall that it was after Paul and Barnabas parted company in their ministry together that God was able to use Paul to return to the cities that he had previously visited to strengthen their faith while Barnabas took John Mark to spread the gospel in a different direction (Acts 5:36-41). Both men continued on in their ministry but with different partners and in different regions of the world. Perhaps God was working behind the scenes to insure that the Gospel message would be taken even farther in a shorter period of time than it would have been taken should the two men have remained together. When such partings between Christian friends does occur we want to be certain that we do so without causing hurt feelings or spreading gossip or slander and asking others to choose sides (Colossians 3:13). Such behaviors do not bring honor to the name of the Lord.

Sometimes friendships change when life dynamics change. Changes such as receiving a promotion, getting married, having a baby, or taking on added responsibility at church or within the community may mean that the time once given to a friendship is now limited. As a result we may be unable to meet the expectations and needs of the previously established friendship.

Each of the above listed scenarios is an example of a situation in which an otherwise healthy friendship will either need to be redefined and restructured or will come to its natural end. Most fearfully wonderful women are able to allow these friendships to run their course and are thankful for the time in which the other person was a part of her life and shared her journey. There are, however, other less healthy and more harmful situations that will require that a relationship be terminated (Proverbs 6:16-19). These endings can be much more stressful and difficult. Examples might be a friendship with someone who has become too demanding or is jealous of our relationships with others. A friendship with someone who criticizes, disrespects or belittles us should also be ended. Friendship with someone who has lied to us or who has violated our trust may have to end if the two of us cannot be reconciled. Likewise friendships with anyone who is selfish, inconsiderate or uncaring may become emotionally draining and will have to end. Remember, the goal of any friendship should be to edify and encourage us into being the best fearfully wonderful woman of God possible (1 Thessalonians 5:11-12). Any friendship that does not meet those requirements must be prayed about and carefully evaluated. The shared relationship actually may not be a friendship at all and could be very unhealthy and destructive for all involved.

✴ ROADSIDE REFLECTIONS:

- Before we begin this next section of actually labeling some unhealthy relationship types, are there relationships in your life that you need to mend? Do you need to go to a sister and re-establish correct communication?

- Are there friendships of which you need to let go? What do you think is driving your need to hold on to a relationship even after it has begun to sour?

- Have you allowed some barriers of protection to be removed or ignored in a particular relationship and now as a result that relationship has become unhealthy?

- How will you begin to make positive steps to repair or to remove yourself from these unhealthy entanglements?

- How do we sweeten a relationship that has begun to sour before it reaches that point?

MANIPULATORS, MARTYRS, MARROW SUCKERS AND OTHER THINGS THAT GO BUMP IN THE NIGHT

Often those of us who openly identify ourselves as Christians will become a target for other people's unhealthy behaviors. This is due in part to the fact that emotionally damaged or spiritually troubled people are drawn to the Jesus that they see in us and without consciously realizing it are seeking His healing touch through us (Mark 2:17, Luke 4:23). This can be a powerful opportunity for ministry if we are equipped to successfully lead these people to the Lord. The danger arises in such relationships when we allow our patient long suffering and Christian forgiveness to be manipulated into ungodly emotional soul ties. Unhealthy and co-dependent relationships have the potential to develop if we are not cautious with people exhibiting troubling behaviors in their interactions with us. We can avoid these unhealthy relationships by being certain that boundaries are clearly defined and respectfully maintained within our relationships with these often needy and hurting people.

At other times we may find ourselves in the middle of an unhealthy relationship because we ourselves have an area of our being that needs deeper healing and we have entered into this relationship seeking to fill a void or a need that only God can fill. The result will be either the failure to establish healthy boundaries at the beginning of the relationship or allowing our boundaries to be violated due to our emotional or psychological need. God created us as social beings with a desire to interact and to be in fellowship with Him as well as with other human-beings (Genesis 2:18, Genesis 17:7, Exodus 6:7, Exodus 29:45). However, if we are not trained to recognize the true character of others we can be easily deceived and entangled in relationships that have the potential to be harmful for us.

In his book; Safe People: How to Find Relationships That Are Good for You and Avoid Those that aren't, Dr. Henry Cloud outlines a few unhealthy characteristics as identified by God of people with whom He was seeking a relationship. Perhaps we could avoid harmful entanglements in our lives by limiting or avoiding associations with people who display these troubling character traits in addition to checking for these characteristics within ourselves. Dr. Cloud's initial list is taken directly from scripture and includes:

- Far away or detached- Isaiah 29:13

- Perfectionistic , critical or proud- Deuteronomy 8:14, Psalms 36:2

- Unfaithful- Joshua 22:16

- Unloving- 1 John 4:20

- Judgmental or critical- Romans 2:1

Outlined below are a few unhealthy and destructive behaviors, the manner in which they are typically expressed, and some examples drawn from scripture of people operating under their influence. These character traits are all manipulative or deceitful in their aspirations, are most often covert and insidious, and are derived from the old sinful nature (Ephesians 4: 22-32). As such, these behaviors are not of God but are direct opposites or counterfeits to how the Spirit of God manifests and works within a person's life. Upon examination of these categories, we may discover that many of the people with whom we interact possess proficiency in one or more of these skill sets and that the boundaries between the categories are often overlapping or flexible. Such behaviors should not be tolerated in any of our friendships and should be confessed as well as dealt with if found to be present within ourselves. These deceptive and manipulative behaviors have the potential to cause emotional, psychological, spiritual and even physical illness and would limit a person's capacity to enter into healthy relationships until that person receives healing and deliverance for whatever aspect of their person is broken or wounded and is prompting their unhealthy emotional response.

- **Manipulators**

We must each remember that friendship is designed to be the **voluntary** sharing of our life with another person and cannot be developed or maintained out of coercion, guilt, fear or some other form of manipulation. Any relationship that is being kept together due to physical threat, sexual or emotional manipulation and enticement, gift giving, or flattery is one that is based upon manipulation . Such relationships are dishonest in content and ungodly in nature (James 1:14-16, 1 John 2:15-17). Every action of a manipulator is of selfish intent and manipulative relationships are based upon using others without regard to obtain a selfish goal.

Healthy relationships can quickly dissolve into manipulative ones if we are not careful. For example, perhaps in an earlier trusting friendship one friend confided something personal in nature such as a dark secret or something damaging from her past. A manipulator will use this knowledge of that secret to keep the other person enmeshed in the relationship by threatening to expose the secret. Manipulators will often respond with wrath, pouting, emotional withdrawal or threat of bodily harm and even suicide when confronted or disappointed by another.

A Biblical example of a manipulator would be Potiphar's wife who used sexual enticement to try to manipulate Joseph to sin. When he refused her advances she then used false accusations, racial slander and jealousy to manipulate her husband to anger and to prompt him to have Joseph unjustly imprisoned (Genesis 39:6-19). Other examples would include Jacob's deception of Esau to steal his rightful birthright away (Genesis 25:29-34) and the beheading of John the Baptist by King Herod as a result of his step daughter's sexual enticement and trickery (Mark 6:14-29).

We can avoid relationships with manipulators by speaking up swiftly when we perceive inappropriate behavior or invasion of our boundaries by another person. It is important not to disclose personal information too early in a relationship and to avoid becoming intimate too quickly. As fearfully wonderful women of God, we must stand firm in our personal values and convictions to avoid being enticed into sin and confess and repent quickly when we fall.

- **Martyrs**

Martyrs love manipulators and manipulators gravitate to martyrs. This is due to a Martyr's need to be needed or appreciated and a manipulator's need to coerce and to control others. Martyrs are easy to control because they often enjoy being manipulated and interpret jealousy, possessiveness and other forms of coercion as signs of deep love and emotional connectedness. Relationships between martyrs and manipulators are symbiotic: that is to say, both parties have needs met through the relationship but do so in unhealthy ways. Martyrs feed off of manipulators and vice-versa in the same way that a bird picking bugs feeds off the back of the hippo upon which it rides. The hippo gets cleaned and the bird gets fed but we cannot say that the two animals are good companions to each other. The bird is in the relationship to meet its needs without regard for the Hippo while the Hippo enjoys having a clean back but does not consider the bird as he moves about from location to location.

Forever the victims, martyrs will often lie and tell you what they think you want to hear as well as overstate their sacrifice or selfless giving to the relationship. They escape responsibility for their actions by pleading to be misunderstood, mistreated and helpless in almost all situations. Martyrs will appear to freely give up their true feelings and opinions in deference to others and will seem never to argue or stand up for themselves. Do not be misled. These actions are self-serving and are a means to achieve an alternative or goal. Martyrs seldom have true compassion or empathy for others. They escape responsibility for their actions by pleading to be misunderstood, mistreated and the helpless victim of circumstances beyond their control.

King Ahab was a very wicked man. He had the reputation of being more wicked than all the kings who had ruled before him (1 Kings 16:30). He was arrogant, stubborn and rebellious and he was skilled in the art of manipulating others by playing the martyr. So skilled that he deceived his equally sinful, domineering and cunning wife Jezebel into doing his dirty work for him by causing her to devise a treacherous plan and to commit murder on his behalf.

Ahab had coveted a vineyard owned by Naboth and wanted it for his own (1 Kings 21:1-2). When Naboth would not sell the land that he had inherited, Ahab went to bed and sulked and pouted refusing to eat or to get up until Jezebel felt sorry for him and devised her wicked scheme to steal Naboth's land (1 Kings. 21:5-14). She set into motion an intricate and devious plot by producing falsified documents and then paying two scoundrels to claim that Naboth blasphemed God and the king in their presence (1 Kings 21:5-14). The false witness resulted in the murder by stoning of Naboth and his sons (2 Kings. 9:26). Ahab was then free to claim Naboth's land without charge for himself (2 Kings 21: 15-16).

A cautionary tale for all of us that points to the insidious nature of martyrdom can be found in the story of the two sisters: Mary and Martha (Luke 10:38-42). Martha was a woman who loved the Lord dearly and yet displayed the sinful behavior of a martyr in his very presence. Martha sought to manipulate Jesus's opinion of her sister and of herself and to win favor with Jesus by whining to him that she was doing all the housework while her sister would not help her. Martha even asked Jesus to scold her sister Mary on her behalf (Luke 10:40). The attitude that Martha displayed toward her sister was not influenced by godly love (1 Corinthians 13:5).

It is impossible to be a martyr and to have a servant's heart (Mark 10:45). Focusing on the needs of others and seeking to emulate Christ will keep us from developing the attitude of a martyr (Matthew 25:40, John 3:30). We should also examine the motivation for our behaviors and be certain that we are sincere in our actions and not merely seeking the approval or attention of another (Matthew 6:3-5). Approval seekers can easily become martyrs for a person or to a cause.

We can avoid falling prey to the manipulations of a martyr by refusing to allow our compassion and love for others to enable their helplessness. Fearfully wonderful women of God must learn to avoid being manipulated by someone who seems to fall apart when we do not take care of them. Often times our loved ones will be better served by taking responsibility for their actions and by doing whatever is necessary on their own to meet their obligations or needs. Likewise, we should not be motivated by inappropriate gifts or praise from others or be flattered by someone who has become too dependent upon us.

• **Marrow Suckers**

These desperately needy people are referred to as "marrow suckers" because they will sap all the joy and energy right out of your being if you allow. Relationships with marrow suckers are marked by their constant need to communicate or to connect with their fuel supply as they present a continual stream of problems, tragedies and drama. Many marrow suckers suffer from a fear of abandonment and produce their endless need out of an emotional fear of rejection or need for approval. These people disrespect boundaries of time and schedules and may rationalize their behavior when confronted by insisting that their current distress or need required our immediate attention. Despite their constant dumping of problems on others, marrow suckers fail to receive solicited advice or counsel and will produce myriad excuses for their dismissal of our offered solutions.

Naturally any unhealthy relationship such as one that is filled with too much drama or distress or that becomes a friendship that demands more energy and time than we can offer should be ended. Such friendships quickly become unbalanced and are burdensome (Proverbs 25:17). We may find it difficult to know how to tell the Marrow sucker that their needs exceed our capacity to give at this time. It may also be difficult to suggest that their needs could be better served through counseling with a Pastor or other professional; but if we have taken on too much or are carrying a burden that we are not called to bear, the weight being placed upon us by the marrow sucker will lead to feelings of resentment or entrapment. Our feelings of guilt for being unavailable to them will be manipulated further. We cannot allow our worry over their reaction to our "deserting them" to become the only thing presently holding the relationship together.

A Biblical character who certainly could have developed the traits of a marrow sucker but did not would be the Apostle Paul. Despite his being whipped, beaten and stoned and being unlawfully arrested and falsely imprisoned multiple times Paul trusted God as his provider and counted his suffering as nothing compared to knowing Christ and his fellowship. Paul was content in all circumstances because He knew God was sovereign (Philippians 3:7-10, Philippians 4:11). Paul told Timothy that he knew that the character of the one in whom he entrusted his life was steadfast and secure and that he was unashamed to suffer for Christ's name (2 Timothy 1:12). Even from behind prison walls He instructed other believers to avoid being anxious by presenting their needs to God and allowing His peace to rule in all of life's circumstances (Philippians 4:6).

We can avoid being a marrow sucker by recognizing that others cannot be expected to fulfill our every need and by turning to our creator as our all sufficient provider (Genesis 22:14, 2 Corinthians 12:1-10). The Lord will see us through our difficulties and encourage our faith if we are obedient and are willing to walk it out. He will see us on our way if we dare to trust him and to commit our footsteps to his order (Proverbs 3:5-6). Likewise, focusing on the hurt and needs of those around us will prevent us from dwelling on our own needs and keep our perception of personal suffering in perspective (Philippians 4:8, James 1:2). Phillip Yancey counsels us through his writing that we should not accuse God of being unfair when we suffer and that Jesus left us his life example of bearing the burdens of those whom he touched in his daily life (Yancey, 1996. P. 325).

We can avoid unhealthy relationships with marrow suckers by requiring others to respect our boundaries and by refusing to play God in the lives of those around us by teaching them to take their petitions to God and to exercise their faith. We must also remember to return thanks and to offer praise in the presence of others to bear testimony to the steadfast and gracious provision of God in our own lives (Psalm 136:1-10).

• **Controlling Spirits**

The Holy Spirit is the only spirit to whom God wishes us to release control and He cannot operate freely within a life where a controlling spirit dominates (Romans 8:12-16, Galatians 5:16). Grace cannot operate in the presence of legalism and bondage (Galatians 5:1). While a shepherding or mentoring spirit wants to guide and to encourage; someone who has a controlling spirit has little room for faith and limits God's power as well as grieves the Holy Spirit. He or she cannot trust another and is actually playing God by assuming that they can rule over everything and everyone that is a part of their life. Having a controlling spirit should be considered a form of idolatry or self-worship because it is self rather than God Almighty that rules and resides on the throne of that person's will. Those with a controlling spirit seek to own or to possess other people and to govern the activities and actions of the world around them. They do not respond well to change. Many actually try to manipulate God or to control His actions through a works oriented approach to Him or by offering up self- serving and arrogant prayers (Luke 18:11). Controlling spirits fear any opinion that is contrary to their own and have no tolerance for individuality or freedom of expression in the lives of others. They may be overbearing, highly opinionated, possessive, jealous, perfectionistic, and unyielding in their interactions with others. Controlling spirits believe that their way of doing something and their perspective on an issue is the only correct one. Most of these people are actually very insecure and often their greatest fear is the loss of control or of being discovered as incorrect, not measuring up or being "less than".

A Biblical example of someone with a controlling spirit is King Saul (1 Samuel chapters 10-12). Like many with a controlling spirit, Saul was charismatic, charming and physically attractive. Scripture tell us that King Saul was a handsome man and the peoples' choice for ruler over the land of Israel (1 Samuel 8:4-5). Upon King Saul's ascension to the throne, the prophet Samuel warned the people of Israel that as long as King Saul and the people obeyed and followed the law of God all would be well but that if they or their king failed to obey God and to recognize His sovereignty they would be doomed (I Samuel 12:14-15). Not too long after his initial reign Saul departed from honoring God and grew arrogant and self-assuming (1Samuel 15:10-11). God withdrew his blessing from Saul's throne as He warned and left him to his own demise. Saul became cruel and bitter and suffered from deep depression and vexation. He later became very jealous over David and his popularity forcing David to flee for his life (1 Samuel

19). Saul's jealousy and fear eventually lead him to forsake the law of God altogether as he desperately turned to a medium and to the occult to receive guidance and knowledge regarding his godless future and the impending doom that he now dreaded (Deuteronomy 18:9-12, 1Samuel 28:1-16). In the case of Saul, it certainly was true that pride went before his destruction and that his haughty spirit bought about his fall (Proverbs 16:18).

Godly humility is the best defense against developing a controlling spirit (Isaiah 66:2, Psalm 51:17, Luke 14:11, James 4:10). We can avoid being controlled by someone with a controlling spirit by searching out the truth of the scripture for ourselves, following our own spiritual convictions, recognizing who we are in Christ Jesus and standing up to intimidation and bullying (Psalm 130:13-18, 1 John 3:1-3, 2 Timothy 1:7). She who is free in Christ is free indeed (John 8:36, 1 Corinthians 7:22).

• **Critical Spirits**

In some of our relationships we may discover that one of us is tender or more sensitive while the other is more direct or candid. This is a matter of personality or upbringing and is not always the result of one member of the relationship having a critical spirit. However, if we desire to interact with our fearfully wonderful sisters, our children, our mates and our family members in an attitude of Godly love, then we need to be careful not to tear down or to humiliate them through our criticism (John 13:34-35, Ephesians 4:32, Ephesians 6:4, Hebrews 10:25) . Scripture warns that doing so can cause a serious stumbling block, possibly inflict great pain, and damage another's faith and relationship with God (Matthew 18:6, Romans 4:10-13, 1 Corinthians 11:31, 1Corinthians 13:5, Philippians 2:3).

The spirit of the Lord seeks to edify and to build up while a critical spirit seeks to condemn, to wound or to cripple and to kill (John 3:17, John 10:10, Romans 8:1). The Word of the Lord divides truth from a lie, reproves and exposes sin, and corrects and instructs those under His authority (Hebrews 4:12, 2 timothy 3:16-17). However, all these things are done through the work of the Holy Spirit in an attitude and atmosphere of love (John 14:26, John 16:13, 1Corinthians 2:10, Ephesians 4:15). Someone operating with a critical spirit will often batter and bruise others and stands in judgment of others from their own biased and prejudiced standards. Their criticism is motivated out of selfish needs and operated from a position of spiritual immaturity or insecurity (James 4:11-12). These people are never happy or satisfied and their relationships are marked by bitterness and strife, gossip and slander (James 4:1-6).

People operating with a critical spirit often fail to control their tongues or their tempers (Romans 1:29-32, James 1:26). When life is not going their way, a critical spirit will lash out by finding fault in everything and everyone. They often criticize others out of a need to elevate themselves or to bolster their threatened self-image and feelings of low self-worth. Their judgmental attitude is fueled by constant negativity and often they do not know why they are upset but simply feel the desire to complain. Unhappy critical people often resort to name calling, belittling and unkind comments and remarks, inconsideration of another's feelings and denial of the harm their words are causing others. Their attacks can be wrapped in sarcasm or acid humor and flippantly dismissed by declaring that they were "only joking".

One Biblical illustration for an entire group of people living under the influence of a grace crippling critical spirit would be that of the Children of Israel as they journeyed through the wilderness. Despite the confirmation that God had appointed Moses as their leader and God's miraculous provision of their escape from Pharaoh through him; they began grumbling against Moses almost immediately after their departure (Exodus 14:10-12). Nothing Moses or God did for them was ever satisfactory or enough (Numbers 11:1). They felt that their lot in life was unfair and that they suffered greatly under God's rule. Never mind that they were walking towards the Promised Land and that God was miraculously providing for their every need. They were tired of walking, wanted water, grew weary of eating God's bland manna, and wanted to go back to Egypt (Numbers 21:4-9). They had lost faith in God's ability to provide and in Moses as their God appointed leader. They refused Moses' counsel and disobeyed God's law. When the people's faith in the God of Abraham, Isaac and Israel was finally overwhelmed by their criticism, bitterness and discontent they constructed their own god and worshiped it in blasphemy to Him (Exodus 32). As a result of their sin, many of the people who started out on that journey of promise died before ever arriving.

In sharp contrast, the scripture contained in 2 Samuel 6:1-23 gives an account of someone who faced and overcame a critical spirit. It is the story of the young King David and his joyful return to the city of Jerusalem after retrieving the Ark of the Covenant from its place of safe keeping within the house of Obed-Edom (2 Samuel 6: 9-12). When David originally obtained the Ark of the Covenant from the house of Abinidab he had placed it there outside of the city for three months but was now going to bring it home to his kingdom and to his people (2 Samuel 6:1-8). David was so overcome with being allowed to usher the physical presence of God Almighty into the midst of his people that he ripped off his royal robes and wearing nothing but his linen ephod, danced before the Lord in total abandon and worship (2 Samuel 6:14-15).

Michal, the daughter of Saul, the now dethroned king of Israel, saw David leaping and dancing from her window perched high above the streets. She was disgusted by his act of foolishness and despised him (2 Samuel 2:16). When he came into the house she openly scolded him and mocked him for lowering or debasing himself as "any vulgar fellow" (2 Samuel 2:20). David's response to Michal's criticism is the one that every fearfully wonderful woman of God should desire to be able to repeat to each of her critics. David knew who he was in the Lord and knew that God had given him favor and had found great pleasure in his worship. He told Michal that he would continue to celebrate the Lord and that he was willing to become even more undignified for the sake of God's glory and praise (2 Samuel 6:21). David did not allow the taunts of Michal or the fear of ridicule and shame to steal his joy or to interfere with his relationship with God. He did not retaliate or respond in kind but left Michal and her attitude up to the Lord (2 Samuel 6:23).

Knowing who we are in Christ Jesus is the best defense against the attacks of a critical and biting spirit. We must know, just as David knew, that God loves us, and that he will never leave us or forsake us (John 3:16-17, Deuteronomy 31:6). If God, the rightful judge, does not condemn us then neither can any man (John 8:10-11). God sees those who laugh at us and ridicule us for the sake of the gospel and he promises to bless us for it (Luke 6:22).

We can avoid having a critical or negative spirit by recognizing the grace of God in our life and by moving in grace towards others. If we truly recognize the blessing of the grace that God has lavished on us then we cannot be ungrateful, bitter or complaining (Matthew 19:29, Ephesians 2:1-10, Ephesians 4:31).

Breaking Free From hurtful Relationships

Ignoring the problems that develop within relationships with martyrs, marrow suckers, controllers, critical spirits and other forms of manipulation will not cause them to go away or bring necessary deliverance and healing.

Continuing in these unhealthy relationships produces excess and heavy baggage that is far too difficult to carry and will result in finding ourselves emotionally, psychologically, physically and spiritually battered and drained. The outcome of our unhealthy enmeshments can be depression, bitterness, anger, resentment and even physical manifestations for our oppression including insomnia, indigestion and overeating. Our negative reactions can begin to infiltrate our daily lives and to negatively affect other relationships including our relationship with the Lord. The more we ignore and give foothold to these sinful behaviors, the stronger their presence and the greater their influence will become within all our daily living.

For the sake of the other person as well as for that of ourselves we are often forced to make the difficult decision to gently and as lovingly as possible end relationships with people displaying these unhealthy traits. If they are not interested or able to seek out help or to get healthy after being made aware of their behavior then we must make some adjustments in our interactions with them. This is especially true if we feel that our own spiritual walk is at jeopardy. Knowing that we have heard the Lord speak clearly regarding his desire for us to step away from a particular relationship and continuing in it for whatever reason is sinful disobedience. That sin will result in establishing a wedge between God and ourselves and will cause our spiritual growth as well as the growth of the other person to be stilted. Letting go of a hurtful relationship and moving forward can have a profound freeing and healing effect in our life as well as in the life of the other individual. Changes in both of our attitudes as well as our physical appearances may actually become outwardly visible once the bonds of the unhealthy relationship are broken. In time, as the Lord applies his grace and unconditional love, each person will be able to move toward forgiveness and reconciliation. Breaking free and getting relationship healing will then serve to strength both testimonies as well as the unity and ministry of the Body of Christ.

COMING OUT OF THE CAMP

Any journey is by definition an act of moving from one's present location in a chosen direction. The word implies going away, making a transition or transporting forward. The first step in moving forward requires that we leave the old behind and venture toward what lies ahead (Philippians 3:13-14). Newness must be welcomed and change embraced in order for progression to occur. Transportation requires transition.

Our journey through life here on earth is lived out through a series of transitions and changes. Those transitions will include our relationships as well as our sense of connectedness to others. As we move through our lives there will be seasons of rich friendships intermingled with periods of isolation. As we grow up into all that God has created in us sooner or later He will call us to come away with Him into a period designed to be a time of preparation, refining, and deeper revelation (Psalm 4:3, Mark 1:17). It has always been part of God's routine to walk together with His creation. From the beginning He would come to the Garden of Eden to walk in the evening midst with His first man, Adam (Genesis 3:8). God was deeply saddened when Adam and Eve hid themselves away and ran from His presence after they had sinned. He desired fellowship and intimacy with His beloved creation. He is saddened still today when we dread or fear His call and run from His desire for time in solitude with us. God has set each of us apart for himself (Exodus 20:4, Jeremiah 1:1-4, Mark 9:2, 2 Corinthians 6:17 1 Peter 2:9).

Living a life of faith can be a real battle. Being an alien or an outsider isn't always the most comfortable way to live. Learning to trust and to patiently wait for God to reveal His plan can be quite difficult some days. As fearfully wonderful women of God, we must each remember that faith is a walk and growth is a process. No journey is complete before it is done! (Profound, huh?) Yet so often the Children of God are like the children in the back seat of the family station wagon with our, "Are we there yet?" and our "What's taking so long?"

There are many examples of leaders in the Bible being called away for a time of separation or preparation before embarking upon a new calling or a new ministry. The Apostle Paul went away for many years into solitude in Arabia after his miraculous conversion experience on the road to Damascus (Galatians 1:16-17). John the Baptist spent time in the wilderness away from crowds and cities (Mark 1:4). Queen Esther was separated from her people and set in position within the King's courts in order to accomplish God's plan for saving his chosen people from savage slaughter (Esther 2:2-4, 4:15-16). The Prophet Elijah was a solitary man who spent a great deal of time alone with his God (1 Kings 19:1-8, 2 Kings 1:1-6) and Moses went up Mount Sinai by himself to meet with God and to receive His covenant commandments (Exodus 24:12). While it is true that Joshua, Aaron and some of the other elders of the tribes went part of the journey up the mountain with Moses, eventually God called him to come up alone to meet Him in the cloud (Exodus 24:13-18). Even the Lord Jesus himself went out into the wilderness for a time of testing and preparation before beginning his earthly ministry (Luke 4:1-14). He continued the discipline of withdrawing to solitude for prayer and meditation throughout his earthly life (Luke 5:15). If Jesus is our model and example then we must be prepared for times of isolation and separation in our lives as well. We should count it a sincere honor when God desires to use us for His service and in preparing us for His ministry He separates us out to commune alone with Him.

Every fearfully wonderful woman can expect to experience at least one such "calling away" or time of separation in her lifetime (Song of Solomon 2:10). Because God loves every fearfully wonderful one of us and desires for us to know Him in his fullness and to value our relationship with Him above all others; He will initiate times in our lives that can serve to draw us closer to him and to deepen our intimacy with Him. He will remove anyone and anything that impedes our dependency upon Him or quenches our desire for Him. The periods of isolation and separation that we experience in our journey have purpose in God's ultimate plan for us. These times should be embraced as times for growth and development because they offer us opportunity to prove our God as all sufficient, ever present and ever faithful. He draws us close to himself to increase our courage, strengthen our faith, augment our power and broaden our knowledge of Him.

Being alone with God on the mountain top allows us to see things from his viewpoint. It is there on His holy hill that He keeps us tucked securely under his wing until He has completed the healing and equipping that we need before being sent forth on our new mission (1 Kings 17:1-3). Being alone with God as we walk through the valleys of difficulty or the muddled fog of uncertainty teaches us to get quiet and still and to listen for the Shepherd's voice to lead us. When we are still, God is free to move on our behalf. When we are silent, God is able to speak in His still small whisper. Often times that mighty thing that is accomplished within us as we are drawn into the secret places could not have been accomplished in the public square.

Just as the Israelites experienced a wilderness as they moved from being enslaved in Egypt to actually receiving the fulfillment of God's Promised Land; so too will all ambassadors go through a time of testing and stretching as we follow Christ until we reach our final destination. Such times away with God should not be dreaded and viewed as periods of dryness or of desert. Being alone with God is never intended to be lonely. Even the most vast and most arid of all deserts is found to be teeming with life upon closer examination. Digging deeply enough into the dry, hot sand will reveal an underground artesian stream of living water. If we discipline ourselves to use these times of separation to dig more deeply into the truth of God's word and to focus on the assurance of His promises and the holiness of His character we may find our wilderness experience to be an oasis of refreshment and renewal. We may find a source of great power and strong faith revealed within us and receive a clarity of vision that can only be derived from our willingness to embrace private, solitary time spent at the feet of Jesus(Luke 10:38-42).

We must not allow our times of separation to become wide deserts of dryness or wildernesses of wandering and frustration. Recall that as the Children of Israel made their way from the bondage of Egypt to the Promised Land flowing with milk and honey they spent far too much time in bitterness and discontent in the wilderness. What should have been a two week journey became a forty year trek of misery, murmuring, doubt and complaint (Deuteronomy 1:2, Exodus chapters 15- 17). The people complained that Moses had lead them out into the wilderness to kill them with hunger and then later of thirst (Exodus 16:3, Exodus 17:3). They complained that God had abandoned them and many said it would have been better if they had remained in Egypt in bondage and slavery than to have followed after God toward their inheritance (Numbers 14:2-4). Oh, how we need to be careful that such murmuring and complaining does not enter our spirits or come from our mouth when God desires to call us away into a time of solitude and testing. God was with the Children of Israel to guide them and to meet their every need. If they had trusted Him to be sufficient and focused on his presence perhaps the purpose for their time of solitude would have been accomplished more quickly and they would have walked into their inheritance sooner. As followers of Christ we should relish our time of fellowship with Him and be honored that the Lord waits for us desiring to share of himself with us and to be gracious to us (Isaiah 30:18). What other human relationship or earthly activity could be of greater value or deeper benefit to any of us than to sit at the feet of Jesus and to meet with God face to face (Philippians 3:8) ?

ROADSIDE REFLECTIONS:

- We must remember that we are called the "body of Christ" for a reason. None of us is supposed to be the Lone Ranger. We are to walk together, to be joined together with Christ as our head and leader and to contribute our part to the whole. We can make this journey of a life time much more enjoyable and much easier if we will learn to call upon each other for encouragement, strength and a little laughter to pull us through. Do you delight in the presence of other fearfully wonderful women of God?

- Don't you just feel great when you finally obey the Lord in a matter that He has been discussing with you? I don't understand why I hesitate to obey the one who created me, loves me unconditionally and knows what is best for me... but I do. Sometimes it's out of doubt, other times its fear and still other times it is straight out selfish rebellion and stubborn sin. Sometimes I think that what He is asking of me is too hard. Other times God's requests seem irrational and make no sense. (Rather like God telling Moses to go back to the land where he is wanted for murder and to stand up to the ruler or like telling Noah to build an ark, or like instructing Peter to fish at the wrong time of the day without having the proper equipment.) But the truth is that God has promised that obedience always brings blessing. He doesn't promise that it will be easy. He doesn't promise that others will agree or that it will make sense. He doesn't even promise that we will get what we want. (Which in and of itself we might see later is a blessing). But He does promise that obedience <u>always</u> brings blessing.

- Is there a relationship matter in which you need to be obedient? Are you willingly surrendering your freedom in the Lord to another's legalism? Do you need to break ties with an unhealthy relationship in which you remain for unhealthy reasons?

- Are there characteristics of your person that you need to heal or to confess in order to avoid attracting martyrs, manipulators, marrow suckers or other joy stealing people to your life?

- Do you need to confess having been critical or controlling in a relationship? Have you been manipulative in your interactions with another?

- And finally, do you want to go back to Egypt, or are you longingly watching others dance around the golden calf when God is calling you to come away with Him? Will you surrender and go away with Him for a time for greater preparation? Are you ready for the journey of a lifetime?

CHAPTER 12

What a Friend We have in Jesus

Each fearfully wonderful woman of God is on a journey. She is a traveler and not a settler. She is an ambassador on the royal assignment of a heavenly king. Her mission will take her through many valleys and deserts and along diverse pathways and up steep and winding trails. At points she will travel swiftly over pleasant and level terrain; while other paths will require a more measured and accurate cadence to avoid the jagged rocks and treacherous ledges of her climb. Some legs of her journey will provide a throng of companions with whom to laugh and to share. These wide and joyful paths of festivity and dance will be intermingled with narrow roads that seem less brightly lit and somewhat desolate or sorrowful. Regardless of her path and of where her journey takes her; every fearfully wonderful woman of God can claim as her greatest assurance the knowledge of this one thing: that each and every step she takes, whether joyful or toilsome, heavy or light, has been ordered by God and is attended by all of heaven's host (Psalm 37:23, Psalm 119:133). Even while walking the most desolate of pathways, she is never alone (Hebrews 13:5). Jesus walks with her.

How beautiful, how wonderful, and how powerful to know that Jesus walks with us every step of life's journey. Jesus is the life time friend who will never leave us or forsake us. We are secure in our journey because we trust in the one who has been ahead and knows what is and is yet to come (Revelation 1:8). He is our Alpha and our Omega. He was there at our journey's conceptualization and will see it through to the very end (Philippians 1:6). His every word speaks into being those secret things that eyes have not seen nor has any ear heard (1 Corinthians 2:9-10). We rest secure in his knowledge of the path that lies ahead and know that his pathway is the way of life (Proverbs 12:28, Jeremiah 29:11).

We are at peace along life's pathways because our companion is the very Prince of peace. His name is Peace (Isaiah 9:6). It is he who reaches deep beneath the tension and stress of the water's tumultuous surface to call up the still dead calm of the sea's tranquility (Mark 4:35-40). In the same manner, Jesus speaks to the howling wind and quiets the storm of fear and doubt that may be raging within us. The peace that Jesus imparts to us is like no other (Isaiah 54:13, John 14:25). It is the peace that defies all human understanding that now sustains us (Philippians 4:7).

We find comfort in the presence of Jesus for He himself is our provision of rest and relaxation (Matthew 11:28). He is the fulfillment of the promised Canaan rest to the children of his covenant (Joshua 21:43-45, Hebrews 4:8). His steps are steps of leisure for his earthly toil is complete. With Christ walking beside us there is no need for rushing forward, no fretting, no fear of anticipation. Our journey can occupy all the time that it requires. We rest in his Triumph (John 19:30, Hebrews 4:9-10). We overcome through Him (Revelation 12:11).

We are wholly accepted and unconditionally loved while being held in his strong arms (John 3:17, Romans 5:1, 1 John 3:1-3). No one ever has or ever will show us greater love than Jesus does (John 15:13). Therefore we have no need for feelings of inadequacy. Our Father finds great joy and pleasure in us (Psalm 104, Zephaniah 3:14, 17). He sees us as perfect through the blood sacrifice of his beloved Son Jesus and we are a showcase of his strength and of his beauty (1 John 3:21, 2 Corinthians 3:4, Hebrews 3:6, Hebrews 4:16). Christ's love has redeemed us from all curses and His love will never fail us (1 Corinthians 13:8, Galatians 3:13). The Word of God has settled that (Psalm119:89).

In Jesus' eyes we are fully equipped and totally capable (Philippians 2:13). In him, we lack nothing (Psalm 34:9, James 1: 2-4). He meets our every need and is our faithful provider (Romans 11:36, Philippians 4:14-19). When we do his will and walk in his way we are blessed and our work bears fruit like that of a well planted tree (Psalm 1:1-3, James 1:25). He gives us grace sufficient for every test and power to defeat any foe (2 Corinthians 12:9, 1 John 4:4).

As fearfully wonderful women of God, we are the body of Christ. Our enemies have no power over us (Romans 12:21). Jesus has delivered us from the evils of this world and because of his great love no evil can overtake us or either our dwelling place (Galatians 1:4, Psalm 91:10). He has provided angels to minister over us and to keep us safe and a shield of faith to stop every enemy attack (Psalm 91:11, Ephesians 6:16). The devil flees from us when we call out the name of Jesus (James 4:7). We have no fear or want for our Shepherd is with us to lead, guide and protect us all the way home (Psalm 23:2-4). When he comes back to get us, we will dwell together with Him forever and ever in our heavenly home (Psalm 23:6, 1Thessalonians 4:17). There He will reign forever in justice and in righteousness (Isaiah 9:6-9).

While every fearfully wonderful woman of God's ultimate destination is that of her heavenly home in the eternal presence of her creator; each footstep of her journey will also move her ever closer toward the wholeness, wellness, contentment and fullness of joy that can only be found walking with Jesus. What a friend we have in Him. There is none other more precious than He.

CHAPTER 13

Bibliography

Adeney, Miriam. A Time for Risking. Priorities For Women. Portland, Oregon: Multnomah Press, 1987.

Ash, Russell. *The Top 10 of Everything (pp. 112-113.)* London, England: Endeavor House/ Octopus Publishing Group, 1997.

Ash, Russell. *The Top Ten of Everything.* London, England: Hamlyn, 2009.

Brooten, Bernadette. "Junia... *Outstanding Among the Apostles*". A Catholic Commentary on the Vatical Declaration. New York: Paulist Press, 1997

Buber, Martin. *Moses.* Amherst, NY: Prometheus Books, 1988.

Cargil, Timothy B., et. Al. *The Life and Times Historical Reference Bible: A chronological Journey through the Bible, culture and History.* Nashville: Thomas Nelson Publishing, 1997.

Cloud, Henry. *Safe People: How to Find Relationships That Are Good for You and Avoid Those That Aren't.* Michigan: Zondervan, 1995.

Cloud, Henry and Townsend, John. Boundaries: *When to Say YES, When to Say NO, To Take Control of Your Life.* Michigan: Zondervan, 1992.

Corley, Kathleen. *Private Women, Public Meals.* Peabody, MA: Hendrickson, 1993.

Maclaren, Alexander. *Expositions of the Holy Scripture: Romans and Corinthians.* Volume 24. London: Hodder and Stoughton, 2003.

Rabey, Lois Mowday. *Women of a Generous Spirit. Touching others with life-giving love.* Colorado Springs: Water book Press, 1998.

Radin, Max. *The Life of the People in Biblical Times.* Philadelphia, PA: Jewish Publication Society, 1948.

Summerville, Geri. The National Campaign to Prevent Teen Pregnancy: Public/Private venues. Annie E. Casey Foundation. www.aecf.org/, 2006

Townsend, John. *Hiding from love: How to Change the withdrawal Patterns that Isolate and Imprison* You, Colorado Springs, CO: Nav Press, 1991.

Townsend, John. Boundaries: *When to Say YES, When to Say NO, TO Take Control of Your Life.* Michigan: Zondervan, 1992.

Ward, Kaari. *Jesus and His Times.* Pleasantville, NY: The Reader's Digest Association, Inc., 1987.

Yancey, Phillip. *Where Is God When It Hurts?* Michigan: Zondervan, 1996.

Zodhiates, S.T. *The Complete Word Study New Testament: Bringing the Original Text to Life.* Great Britain: AMG Publishers, 1992.

Zodhiates, S.T. *The Complete Word Study Old Testament: Bringing the Original Text to Life.* Great Britain: AMG Publishers, 1994.

Cindee would love to come share with the fearfully wonderful women of your community. For additional information regarding Cindee's speaking and teaching ministry or to join in the conversation with other members of the encourage entourage please visit her website at: fearfullywonderfullywoman.webs.com or contact Cindee directly at *fearfullyfemale@gmail.com.*